this is

where

we

came in

.

THIS IS
WHERE
WE
CAME IN
...

essays by

LYNNE SHARON SCHWARTZ

COUNTERPOINT

BERKELEY

Library of Congress Cataloging-in-Publication Data
Schwartz, Lynne Sharon.
This is where we came in : intimate glimpses / Lynne Sharon Schwartz.
pages cm
ISBN 978-1-61902-246-1
1. Schwartz, Lynne Sharon. 2. Authors, American—20th century—
Biography. I. Title.
PS3569.C567Z46 2014
813'.54—dc23
[B]
2013029182

ISBN 978-1-61902-246-1

Cover design by Natalya Bolnova

Counterpoint Press
1919 Fifth Street
Berkeley, CA 94710
www.counterpointpress.com

Printed in the United States of America
Distributed by Publishers Group West

10 9 8 7 6 5 4 3 2 1

Contents

THIS IS
WHERE
WE
CAME IN

. . .

You Gotta Have Heart

CIGARETTES

A pack of Vantage containing two cigarettes was in my coat pocket when I arrived at the hospital. It was a bitter morning in late December. The angiogram was scheduled for eleven o'clock, at least I had been told to be there at eleven o'clock, but it didn't take place until three in the afternoon. I made a scene over this at hourly intervals, first arguing with the receptionist in the waiting room, then insisting on being admitted past the swinging double doors behind which others before me had disappeared, to confront whoever was in charge back there. Just because they were the authorities, the medical bureaucracy, I wasn't going to be a meek cipher in their hands. I would begin this journey in the right spirit.

But no matter how vehemently I railed against the injustice and lack of consideration, the angiogram didn't take place until three o'clock.

The surgeon had advised that I stay at the hospital after the angiogram, since the heart surgery would begin around six the next morning: why go home merely to get up in the middle of the night and return? This seemed sensible and I agreed. My plan was that once the angiogram was over—I understood you had to lie still for an hour or so afterwards—assuming I survived, I would go out with my husband for a cup of coffee and to smoke what would be my last cigarettes for quite a while. Maybe forever. Again, assuming I survived. Whenever doctors or nurses lean over my body preparing to insert something in a place not designed to be penetrated, I feel endangered. During the angiogram, they would be making a hole in my groin and threading a tube straight up to my heart; it sounded like an unwieldy as well as unnatural procedure, but many before me had survived it and most likely I would too.

While it was in progress, though, I had my doubts. I wasn't completely unconscious; I had enough awareness to hear the older doctor telling the younger one—a very young doctor, his bare face sticking out of the plastic shower cap was cherubic—what to do, how to guide the tube inside me, and so on. I said, "Why so much instruction? Are you actually teaching him how to do this on me?" The older doctor laughed, ha-ha. "No, of course he knows how to do it."

I didn't want to distract them from the lesson, and so I desisted. Also, I really wasn't up for a dialogue; I was too entranced by the drug. I'm not sure what they gave me—if I were, I'd try to get a prescription —but it was something that leaves you half awake and aware, and yet everything happening to your body, as well as the people working on it, seems at a great remove. So close and yet so far. Something unnatural is happening to you, but it's painless, and anyway, "you" are not the same singular entity as before: there's the body that belongs to you (who else?) and then there's your dimmed consciousness, looking on from afar. A great drug, but it wears off quickly.

Instead of carrying out my plan of the cup of coffee and cigarettes afterwards, I found myself being led into an elevator by an orderly, deposited on a floor, and assigned a room, a rather nice private room: a luxury floor. The room had the usual hospital paraphernalia and TV protruding from the wall like a hunter's stuffed moose head, but it also had the mildly pleasant, expectant, scentless air of a hotel room, and that was how I intended to treat it. I began getting out of the grotesque hospital gown—white with little blue circles, not dots but donut-like circles, little O's. Later I found that this garment, whose only accommodations to the shape of the human body were enormous sleeves and a string to be tied at the neck, also came in sky blue with no circles.

I can't help wondering if there is some reason—economy, perhaps, or mere thoughtlessness?—why these hospital gowns have to be quite so humiliatingly ugly. I know they have to be open so that the body within is fully accessible to the professionals who will handle it, but must it be ugly besides? Adding insult to injury, so to speak? Would it cost so much more to use the services of a designer, maybe not someone first-rate like Donna Karan or Ralph Lauren—that would be an extravagance—but some young person just starting out who'd be grateful for the work? It would be only a onetime thing.

I was reaching for my street clothes when a nurse came in to the room. "What are you doing?" she asked, gazing at me and my husband, who sat in one of the pink plastic chairs.

"Getting dressed," I said.

"You're supposed to leave the gown on," she said.

"My surgery isn't until tomorrow morning and it's not even six yet. We're going out to get a cup of coffee." Despite my pose of bravado, I knew enough not to mention the cigarettes.

She was no Sue Barton but a stern-looking nurse of the old school: stocky, short hair in a mannish cut, sharp voice, no nonsense. "You're not going anywhere. This is your room. You'll stay here until they call for you."

"I beg your pardon," I said. "The surgery isn't until tomorrow, as I said. The angiogram is over. There's nothing you need me for. I'm going out. I promise I'll return for dinner," I said with a little chuckle, to lighten the situation. I didn't want to make this a fight over my civil rights, or rather I did—but without being pompous, as such fights are liable to be. I tied my sneakers as I spoke.

"You don't understand," she said, a bit more gently, as if indeed the rules hadn't been explained to me properly. "You are a patient."

My mother used to tell me that I had no patience. She also used to say, during my minor childhood illnesses, that I was a terrible patient, I suppose meaning fretful, demanding and impatient. Maybe because I've been labeled impatient, I've always disliked the homophonic connection between the noun *patient*, the sick person, and the adjective *patient*, the character trait. They come from the same Latin root, meaning suffering or enduring, and it's easy to see why that root branched out in the two directions and parts of speech. But that doesn't mean that a patient necessarily is or ought to be patient, that is to say, according to the dictionary definition, "enduring pain, trouble, affliction hardship, etc., with fortitude, calmness, or quiet submission." Certainly it makes practical sense to endure one's ailment with fortitude and calmness (not that practical sense ever played a large part in determining my attitudes). But must a patient also endure with "quiet submission" the thousand and one well-documented indignities of hospital life? I would think a patient's patience is already being sufficiently tried by illness; she shouldn't be expected to muster still more reserves of patience for those indignities. Rather it's the doctors and nurses who should be patient with the already patient patient.

All the same, after my husband went home and I began anticipating the events of the next morning, the fighting spirit deserted me. I was a patient. I put on the hospital gown, ate the hospital dinner, and settled into bed with a fat Henning Mankell mystery. All that was missing was a cigarette, one of the two in my coat pocket, but I didn't dare. It was a good thing I didn't, because the nurse entered and seemed pleased to find I had surrendered like a chastised child. She gave me a stack of papers to sign granting the hospital permission to do with me as it would, and I signed without really reading them, just a quick glance. I was in no mood to contemplate whatever I was agreeing to. Then she gave me a thick folder full of information about hearts and heart surgery, complete with diagrams and charts. "This literature may be helpful to you," she said. "It will familiarize you with your surgery, and with what goes on in the heart in general, how it functions and how to take good care of it."

I accepted the folder politely but had no intention of spending what might be my final hours reading its contents. In my heart I was thinking, So this "literature" will tell me what goes on in the heart? As if I didn't know! I'd spent years of my life reading about the heart. There was little I didn't know. *The Heart Is a Lonely Hunter. The Heart of the Matter. The Heart of Matter. In the Heart of the Country. In the Heart of the Heart of the Country. A Simple Heart. Near to the Wild Heart. The Mortgaged Heart. Heart of Darkness. Change of Heart. Crimes of the Heart. Habits of the Heart.* The heart has its reasons, Pascal said.

THE SURGEON

Weeks before the surgery, I meet the surgeon for the first time. He is a young man, quite good-looking in the common way of well-bred American white males, so common I barely notice them: dark hair, squarish face, neatly shaped features. Charlie Sheen, say, or the younger Tom Cruise. Courteous manners. He explains the "procedure." I ask him what kind of valve, animal or artificial, he will use to replace my faulty one. I thought I'd have some say in the choice once I was apprised of the advantages and disadvantages of each, but now that we sit here contemplating the surgery, I realize he's not the kind of doctor who will welcome my input; he is most definitely the decider, as George Bush used to say, and that's okay with me because I don't really have an opinion. He says animal.

"What kind of animal? A pig?"

"No. A horse."

There is a pause, as I consider horses as opposed to pigs. "This may sound like a silly question," I say, "but isn't a horse valve a little large for me?"

He laughs. I made him laugh, quite unintentionally. There was a saying we had back in Brooklyn, that some girls think they're hot shit because they can make a man laugh in bed, the joke being that this is pretty easy to do, within the range of almost anyone. "We don't use the entire valve," he says. "We make a valve from material in the horse's heart."

Oh. What about those horses? Is it like organ transplants—someone young and healthy is in an auto accident and their intact, barely used organs are rushed to a patient who needs them? No, I doubt it. Horses don't get into auto accidents. Are they horses who've outlived their usefulness and are put out to pasture, like Black Beauty, whom I wept over in adolescence, to spend the remainder of their lives at ease, as in a nursing home? (Though people in nursing homes tend to decline and die faster than those cared for at home.) And then the horses die of natural causes but have agreed beforehand to allow their organs to be used for humanitarian purposes? I mean of course that their owners agreed. Perhaps their owners got paid for the heart parts; yes, surely they got paid.

Now that I think of it, sitting here facing the young, generically handsome and self-assured doctor, I actually prefer a horse to a pig, if I have to have some other species inside me. I don't feel fastidious or repelled by the prospect of carrying around a part from another species; after all, we're all in this together, all creatures great and small. Nor am I a snob about animals. But I think most people would allow that horses are more attractive than pigs. As I'm staring at the doctor—a button on his right shirt cuff is loose and dangling, it could fall off any minute—it occurs to me that perhaps Orthodox Jews with a faulty aortic valve would not permit a pig's valve to be lodged inside them. If their doctor opted for a pig, they might protest and insist on a horse—no cloven foot. If no horses were available, those people would have to have an artificial valve. Also I read somewhere that

Orthodox Jews, whose wives and daughters wear wigs covering their natural hair, stopped permitting wigs made of Indian hair. Indian hair is the best hair for wigs, and perhaps the best hair all around, period. There is a thriving business in selling Indian women's hair. But the Orthodox Jews thought that some of the original women's Hindu-ness might have infiltrated into the hair and thus would violate the heads of their new wearers. Well, I'm not an Orthodox Jew, so I needn't concern myself with hair just now, or with the doctor's loose button. Just pigs and horses.

Like a pubescent girl, I love horses. I even rode horses, though not well, in my teen years. My family spent the summers in a bungalow colony in the Catskills, whose aggressive dullness I loathed, but its saving grace was the nearby hotel where you could rent horses and ride around on the dirt roads. My favorite horse was called Brownie, very gentle, and I learned to trot, to post properly, and even to canter, before I got old enough to stay home alone in the summers. In Brooklyn a few times, I rented horses at a stable near Bergen Beach and rode along the ocean. I felt I was in a movie: the surf, the sand, the sky, the horse and me on it. I rode just two or three more times as an adult, and then the equestrienne part of my life was over.

But I do know horses, at least a bit, and I would like to know the provenance of the piece of horse heart about to be lodged in my own: was he or she a farm horse, a police horse, maybe a prize racehorse? I enjoy the races. I've been to the track lots of times, both Belmont and Saratoga, with my husband and friends. Could I possibly be harboring a piece of a horse I've seen in a race, a horse I might have bet on, and won with?

"Okay," I say. "A horse." I'm trying to think of suitable and intelligent questions to ask. "How do you get to the valve? I mean mine, not the horse's."

"We reach in," he says, not exactly tersely, but in a tone that means he doesn't care to elaborate.

We reach in. I've remembered those words ever since as a kind of magic formula, an Open Sesame, as it were. So ominous, so graphic and yet so vague, enigmatic. They reach into me. Me! This man would touch my heart as no man ever had before.

The only other question I have for the surgeon was, Will I die by your knife? and it certainly isn't suitable to ask that. What do I expect? Of course he'll say I'll be fine. He'll probably say, with a confident chuckle, that he's done this hundreds of times, thousands. Later on I thought of many specific and important questions, but at the time, as I confront him before the surgery, my mind is blank. It seems I should know him better than one brief appointment's worth, since he would be opening my chest and handling my heart. And yet he's a virtual stranger. It's like going to bed with someone when all you know about him is his name, if that.

"How long is the recovery period?" I ask as I get up to leave.

"Two weeks," he says.

MILD, SEVERE, CRITICAL

It wasn't as if I was undertaking this surgery under duress, as it may appear from my recalcitrance. No, strictly speaking, I chose it. I'd known about the faulty valve for several years, but at first the cardiologist, a gentle, rotund, clear-eyed youngish man, said the situation was "mild." Unless and until it progressed through "moderate" to "severe," to "critical," at which point it would require surgery, I should forget about it and carry on with my normal life. In that instance, I was more than willing to obey the doctor without question. At this rate, "critical" would not arrive for many years, I thought, maybe so many years that I would already be dead and therefore no surgery would be necessary. I carried on. Until one day after a stress test, the cardiologist directed his steady gaze at me and said the state of the valve had passed "severe" and was near "critical." He strongly recommended surgery. Soon.

"Are you serious?" I said, still panting from the stress test, sitting on the examining table, my legs dangling down. The idea of undergoing surgery had no reality for me, even though I'd seen several members of my family go through it. From my husband's bypass operation six years ago, I knew intimately what open-heart surgery entailed.

"Very serious. If you don't do it, you have a fifty-fifty chance of dying of this in two years."

Aha. Something clicked in my mind as I quickly moved into rebuttal mode. "But that means I also have a fifty-fifty chance of living. So . . ." I shrugged.

"Okay then," he said, his kindly face unchanged. I guess he'd heard every kind of response, even flippant. "Make it four years. Then your chances of dying really improve."

The doctors, I later learned, call invasive surgery an insult. (My husband's doctor referred to his heart surgery as "the second insult." When I asked what was the first, he said, "Birth.") Now I could see the aptness of the term. More than repelled and frightened by the prospect of surgery, I also felt insulted—in advance—especially as I recalled the array of side effects my husband, sister, and brother had experienced. But I didn't want to die in two years, or even four. So I chose to be a patient instead.

THE DEAD

In the two years just before my surgery, two of my closest friends died. They both lived right nearby, Glenda around the corner for twenty years and Rebecca about three blocks west for even longer. Glenda died of a brain tumor, or perhaps it was ovarian cancer that spread to her brain. She died in Australia, where she was born, so I didn't see her in the last few months, only spoke to her on the phone. By the end her voice on the phone sounded like static. Rebecca died of lung cancer. I saw her a lot during that illness, except near the very end, when I called to ask if I could come over and she said, "I love you, dear, but I can't see you." I always was touched when she called me *dear*. I don't find it easy to use endearments, except to children.

We were all writers together. I met Rebecca at Yaddo, a writers' colony, and though I felt slightly intimidated by her—she was very shy, I later learned, and this gave her an air of aloofness—I invited her to take a walk one afternoon. Yaddo is in Saratoga Springs, New York, where the famous horse races take place, and on our walk through a back lane, we passed stables and horses meandering around a meadow, a tranquil scene. Little did I know then, thirty-two years earlier, that one day a piece of horse would prolong my life, though not any of the horses we saw that day—they don't live that long.

After that walk we were good friends for thirty-one years. I met Glenda because I reviewed a book of hers for *Ms. Magazine*. The book, full of bizarre and darkly whimsical happenings, intrigued me; I thought the person who wrote it must be odd and eccentric, and so I went to a reading she gave in an East Side bookstore to check her out. I was hesitant about introducing myself to the author of a book—I hadn't published any books at the time, only short pieces in magazines—but she was approachable and grateful for my review. We discovered that we were neighbors and we too became friends for decades.

I introduced Glenda and Rebecca, and we formed a kind of trio, meeting in the late afternoon in the historic West End Bar near Columbia University to drink and smoke and talk about our work and about life, as had Allen Ginsberg, Jack Kerouac and many writers before us. We three had met as writers and continued that way, although as our lives became enmeshed and our children grew up we talked about everything else under the sun. We were very different but we came to understand one another perfectly because we were intuitive about reading character, the signs of character. Glenda, who was not odd or eccentric in any immediately obvious way, had her Australian accent and spoke in a soft, gentle voice and had impeccable manners, and in that soft, gentle voice she said outrageous and radical things. Rebecca was older and seemed to carry the wisdom of the ages in her head capped by sleek auburn hair shaped like a bowl, but she carried her burden lightly, with wit; she was from Georgia and had a pronounced Southern drawl and a wry skepticism about most things, but a sentimental streak that came out in her love of cats and dogs. There was a spell when I would ride my bike down Riverside Drive first thing in the morning, and I often met Rebecca walking her dog, who she insisted had said a few words and even shed a few tears. Glenda drove a large car and I'd sometimes meet her going to move her car in accordance with the parking regulations, as one must do on the Manhattan streets: she said she had learned to spot people who were about to vacate their parking spaces. She could tell who they were by their purposeful gait and by the way they fiddled with their keys in their pockets, and she followed them.

Sometimes two of us would meet, and I wondered about the combinations of two out of three: for instance, how the two of them sounded and spoke when I wasn't present. The ways I spoke with each of them alone were very different; this was inevitable, given how unlike we were. We resembled three interlocking circles—I'm thinking of the old Ballantine Ale logo, the three circles standing for Ballantine's salient qualities, purity, body and flavor. None of us represented any of those qualities especially, but the design fit. We shared a considerable common area, yet each of us had a large private space of our own.

Anyway, they died, Glenda in 2007 and Rebecca in 2008 and I was bereft. After Glenda died so far away, Rebecca and I felt the lack. Even though our friendship was rich on its own, we would never again know that special interlocking threesome. Then Rebecca got sick and though we never said it aloud, we both knew I would continue with a double loss, missing the particular quality of our friendship, in which we could say anything that occurred to us and neither of us would ever be shocked, and sometimes we need not even say it—a meaningful look could convey volumes. Rebecca was unshockable, and through her I learned to be the same.

So when I went for my heart surgery I thought, I am the last of the three, and maybe this year, the third year, 2009, will be my turn.

As they wheeled me into the operating room, before the anesthetic put me out, I had a glimpse of them in an afterlife that resembled the old West End Bar where we used to meet in the ancient booths, dark and smoky, nursing our drinks of choice: wine, bourbon, and, for me, Diet Pepsi; I was never much of a drinker. They're chatting away. I don't know what the two of them sound like alone, without me, but I do manage to hear a few words in Glenda's gentle, now slightly anxious voice: "Where's Lynne? She's never this late." Then comes Rebecca's deep, bourbon-soaked drawl. "She'll turn up soon. She's very reliable that way."

REHEARSAL

When I first came out of the operating room I was adorned with lots of tubes, like someone who's just come from the Mardi Gras parade in New Orleans, bedecked with colorful necklaces and bracelets: tubes in several orifices and some where there were no orifices to begin with, such as the chest. Over the next few days the tubes were removed, one by one, some with a pop and some with a slither. My tubes were removed by a young Japanese physician's assistant named Elliot, a small doll-like man, delicate and slim as a miniature. I became fond of Elliot: something about his easygoing, competent manner combined with his delicate appearance inspired trust. He listened to my complaints with a benevolent neutrality and often told me not to worry. Usually it's irritating to be told not to worry, but when Elliot said it I didn't mind. He rarely smiled yet appeared serene, and he always explained exactly what he was about to do. With one of the tubes, a catheter, he said he would count, one, two, and then I must take a deep breath while he pulled it out, and that way it wouldn't hurt. One, two, breathe! Okay? I nodded. I breathed at the proper moment and it didn't hurt. Elliot praised me as if I were a kindergartner who had just written the letter *A* for the first time. I was proud of myself. It was a small accomplishment, true, but in my diminished condition, it was prideworthy. I felt so diminished and changed after the surgery that I couldn't take anything for granted anymore.

Pulling out the chest tube was more complicated as well as risky. It required some rehearsal. "We can't let any air get into the pleural cavity where this tube is," said Elliot, "so we have to practice first. You breathe, hold your breath, and I pull. Don't release your breath until I have the tube fully out. Do you understand?" I nodded.

"So we'll have a little rehearsal first," he said.

All this attention gave me a heady feeling, as if I had an important part in a play. As an adolescent I had aspired to be an actress and even studied acting for a while at the Henry Street Playhouse. One of my teachers was William Hickey, who later played, among other roles, a Mafia capo in a popular crime movie, a comedy. My aspirations came to nothing since I had little talent and much reserve. Still, with this in my past and diminished as I felt, the thought of a rehearsal of any kind brought a bit of excitement.

Elliot implied, or I inferred, that if air got into my pleural cavity, something terrible might happen to me. Surely less adept and alert people must have had this tube removed and I'd never heard of any misfortunes resulting. And yet I felt it was a matter of life and death to do it right. "Breathe," said Elliot. "Hold. I pull." I held my breath while he pretended to pull. We rehearsed this two or three times.

"Okay, ready for the real thing?"

I was ready. Breathe, hold, pull. Together we did a perfect job. The final tube. I was on my own.

When he left I had one of those marvelous epiphanies, like little mental orgasms, that unfortunately don't last long. If they did, we might never get back to the world's work. I was staring out at the Hudson River, wide, placid that day, steel gray in a wan sun, and suddenly I was seized by the glory, the miracle of being alive: I'd had that ghastly surgery and survived. It was done, I was blessed. None of the dailiness I'd fretted over before, family problems, work, dealings with banks and institutions, the construction across the street whose dumpsters' groans and beeps woke us at seven a.m., plus the dire state of the world, mattered any more. Compared with the wonder of life itself, those things were small and would sort themselves out. What mattered was that I would continue living. I didn't stop to think about in what condition I would live, too fine a point just then. Simply, as Strether in Henry James's novel *The Ambassadors* cries, "To live, to live!"

This feeling lasted, though not in the full intensity of its first strike, for about two and a half days. By the time I went home to start the labor of recovery, all the daily irritations came back and resumed their usual importance. And a little later on came the fear.

RECREATION

Towards the end of my five-day sojourn in the hospital, when I could walk around comfortably, I looked for entertainment other than staring out the window at the Hudson River from the pink plastic armchair in my room or reading my fat Henning Mankell mystery. I practiced going up and down stairs on the miniature wooden staircase near the nurses' station: it led nowhere, just five steps up and five down with a small platform on top. I made believe I was a political candidate about to deliver a campaign speech to an adoring crowd. I tried hanging out in the waiting room to feel part of the great outside, to hear conversations among civilians, not patients, conversations not about symptoms and procedures but about worldly things, sports, movies, traffic accidents, natural disasters . . .

A pretty fiftyish woman with lots of makeup and bright red hair elaborately carved into in a towerlike pile asked me what I was "in for" and who was my surgeon. When I told her, she grew rhapsodic on the subject of my surgeon, a genius and savior. He had saved the lives of both her mother and her priest in conditions of extreme coronary drama. Furthermore, it had been he, she claimed, who operated so successfully a few years ago on former President Bill Clinton, although owing to hospital hierarchy and public relations, the feat had to be attributed to the head of the department.

What to say to this dubious bit of gossip? "You don't say," I said, using an expression from my childhood I believe I never used before.

The man next to her, whom I recognized as the husband of my new roommate—she had arrived attended by her family in the middle of the night—said, "I was in the living room and my wife was in the kitchen. I heard her calling, but to tell the truth, most of the conversation in the house is between my wife and the dog, so at first I assumed she was talking to the dog. What did that dog do now? But she kept calling, so I figured I better go see. She was lying on the floor groaning. When we got her here we learned her aorta had ripped all the way down her body to her thigh." This sounded almost as gruesome as the murders Henning Mankell had concocted in his very long book.

It was, yet again, my surgeon who had saved her life. When she was brought to my room last night after the surgery, her appearance was not promising. She was quite overweight in her hospital gown, bedecked with tubes as I had been, and her skin was almost as gray as her long, disheveled hair. She coughed all through the night, deep wracking wet phlegmy coughs that seemed to rise from the pit of her stomach and spew upwards like a geyser. At one point I rang for a nurse because the coughing alarmed me: she could die while I lay listening and then I would feel guilty for my inaction. The nurse came and murmured, "That's what happens when you have surgery after a lifetime of smoking."

That might have been me, I thought, given my lifetime of smoking, and I felt a moment of rare gratitude that it was not. Even though smoking wasn't the cause of my nasty valve, by rights I suppose I should have been coughing too. The woman's coughing reinforced the dogma that smoking has terrible effects. But it also suggested that in some cases it might not. I thought of the two cigarettes still in my coat pocket, in the closet of our hospital room. If my roommate weren't so sick we could share them, have our last cigarette together, maybe in the bathroom with the door locked, like ten-year-olds.

The red-haired woman said, "I practically fell to my knees when I saw him after my mother came out of the recovery room. I didn't know how to thank him."

I hadn't seen the surgeon since my operation. He'd seen me but I was unconscious at the time, and I later learned that just after the surgery, he'd referred to my valve as "very nasty." I didn't know whether to feel offended, as at an insult, or to feel pride at having generated something so noteworthy. In any case, I hadn't given a thought to thanking him, which in retrospect seems ungrateful and ungracious. But at that point I was still thinking of him more as my assailant than my savior.

"So how did you thank him?" I asked.

"I'll give you a tip," she said, winking. "He likes Cabernet Sauvignon. By the case."

After a while I left the waiting room and took an exploratory walk down the corridors. I'd been encouraged to walk and for once was glad to follow orders. I like walking, even down a hospital corridor where you peek into rooms and see people in various states of disrepair and wearing charmless cotton gowns.

After my walk I returned to my chair at the picture window overlooking the Hudson and resumed the Henning Mankell mystery in which so many vile murders were described. I'm not an avid reader of mysteries; the only time I read them passionately was when I was around ten or twelve and gorged myself on Agatha Christie, Erle Stanley Gardner and *Ellery Queen's Mystery Magazine*. That quickly passed. But over the last few years, I'd begun listening to books on tape while I puttered and exercised in the morning, and found mysteries ideal for this purpose. Their merits aren't exclusively or primarily literary (although there are exceptions like P. D. James or Walter Mosley), so I needn't be afraid of missing some splendid phrase. The plots kept me going through the tedium of the exercises.

I discovered Henning Mankell on the shelves of a friend's guest room where I stayed every Tuesday night one spring, when I taught a course at Bryn Mawr. This friend, with whom I'd gone to graduate school years earlier, had very exacting taste. She was so learned that for a long period she was head of the English Department at Bryn Mawr, so I assumed anything I found on her shelves would be high-class stuff. I started a Henning Mankell mystery one night and got so absorbed that I asked if I could borrow it for the train ride home and return it the following week.

Henning Mankell is from Sweden, and his detective, Kurt Wallander, lives in a small, dismal Swedish town. Wallander is depressed, like his town. He has lots of personal problems—his divorce; his relationships with his grown daughter and his aging father, an eccentric painter; his insomnia; and so on—besides the distressing murder cases assigned to him. He is often tired, cold, rain-soaked and at odds with his fatuous supervisor. Wallander is an instinctive detective, thorough and painstaking rather than brilliant, and he quickly grew on me.

Mankell writes in short, factual sentences that one by one are not striking, but when strung together become passages of vivid and forceful prose. Prose that's hard to stop reading. I kept the light on over my hospital bed each night, following the crimes and Wallander's team of eccentric detectives, the hunted and the hunters. The story was more grotesque than usual in a Mankell book, which is generally pretty grotesque. It involved a nurse seeking out and killing, in ingenious and sadistic ways, men who had abused and murdered women. Once she found the abusers, she tied them up, placed them in sacks, starved them and subjected them to other lengthy indignities I've managed to suppress. Reading about this treatment in the hospital after having my chest opened up, with people all around me whose chests had been opened up for one reason or another, felt satisfying. The world was full of atrocities, and the motives, benign or malignant, didn't seem to matter much. What mattered was simply the fact of the intrusions—that one person had performed them on a fellow human.

My attitude regarding the surgery was not the conventional, expected or sensible one, that's for sure. It was more childish than adult. I knew this, and yet I clung to my resistance. It felt satisfying, far more so than quiet submission. Weeks after my release, when I met acquaintances or neighbors on the street and told them why they hadn't seen me around, some people responded by saying, Isn't it wonderful, the miracles they can perform these days! Aren't you lucky!, and the like. I wanted to punch them. In some obscure nook of my brain, I knew there was some truth to their words, but I wouldn't acknowledge that nook. There are times I still don't. It wasn't so much their actual words that disturbed me, but the gross ignorance behind them, ignorance of anything other than pure survival. Ignorance of what the newspapers call collateral damage. When listening to news reports of our current wars, I always find the collateral damage aspect the most intriguing. I wish the reporters would examine that damage further—who are these unintended victims whose lives end for no reason other than someone's faulty aim, or being in the wrong place at the wrong time? Why shouldn't their photos, with small intimate bios, appear on the back pages of the *New York Times*, as did those of the victims of the September 11 attacks?

Collateral damage as a result of surgery is quite different, of course. The patient is far from dead. Rather, the patient's entire body is analogous to the nation under siege, and regrettably, individual parts of the body unrelated to the main arena of attack are made to suffer.

The Hippocratic oath enjoins doctors to do no harm. But my surgery did harm; not only the sawing and hammering open of my chest and all that went with it, but the onslaught of fear—called depression by the professionals—that took me by surprise a couple of months later and that allegedly strikes 30 to 40 percent of heart surgery patients. So technically the doctors violated the oath. But of course they must, in order to do their work. Every painful treatment could be considered a violation of the oath. On the other hand, if my faulty valve caused my death within a couple of years (as the sweet-faced cardiologist predicted), and if the doctors had a remedy that could have averted that and yet they withheld it, that too would be doing harm. Arguably even more harm. You can't win: harm is done either way. Again, it's a matter of motives and results, means and ends, a slippery subject. Maybe the problem is with the oath itself, but of course no one would consider rescinding it, because who knows what doctors might do, left to their own devices.

With all this, our fate here in the hospital hinged on the doctors. We revered them and resented them, at least I did. I didn't resent them because they were helping me, as in, No good deed goes unpunished. No, I'd probably resent anyone I had to revere. Reverence is simply not part of my makeup. I dislike hierarchies, though I know they are ubiquitous in the animal kingdom. Long ago I worked for several years as a secretary for a Quaker organization and learned that Quakers don't use titles, even such common ones as Mr. and Mrs. (or now, Ms.). I was instructed, when I typed letters, to address the recipients, no matter how distinguished, by both names, for example, Dear Albert Einstein, or Dear Nelson Mandela. Also, while the secretaries called each other and our own bosses by first names, we addressed all the other executives by their full names. I liked that. I still write letters that way. But I do call doctors Dr., despite the Quakers' practice of full names and feminism's eminently sensible policy: if the doctor calls you Lynne, you call him Joe. I don't want to get that chummy.

I shouldn't have been surprised that the people in the waiting room weren't discussing sports and earthquakes. They were relatives and friends of patients, and like those of us wearing the gowns, they were affected, or afflicted, by the hospital atmosphere, in which nothing is of any importance except living or dying. The awareness of the body's vulnerability, which normally doesn't need constant acknowledgement, is perpetual here. Anyone who ends up in a hospital bed is by definition in danger. No wonder it's hard to focus on anything else.

At least that was so on the cardiac floor; maybe on less serious floors—broken bones, knee replacements, gallbladders—it's different. Here, we've come to be saved, to go on living. And we're rooting for each other, our sisters and brothers ambling through the halls dragging their IV poles, clinging to their slender dancing partner. There's a heartfelt camaraderie, a pure, unambiguous feeling you won't find in many other groups forced together by chance and circumstance. Most of us will probably live to go home—they certainly don't want us dying here—but how long after that?

"YOU WILL SWALLOW THE TUBE"

Less than two weeks after the surgery, I find myself being prepared, in an extremely small room crowded with medical equipment, for a TEE, a transesophageal electrocardiogram: a tube with a tiny camera at the end goes down the esophagus and behind the heart in order to see if there has been any stroke activity back there, any pieces— "grunge matter," one doctor called them—broken off during surgery that traveled to the brain. The TEE, one of several tests for stroke, is happening because a few days earlier, barely back home after my bonding with the anonymous horse, I looked down at the strips of tape bisecting my chest—some strips halfway off, some hanging longer than others, an ungainly tangle of tape—and asked why they were there. I never keep myself in such a messy state. My husband immediately realized, especially after a few more weird remarks, that something had gone wrong in my brain. Next stop, the emergency room of a nearby hospital, not the hospital where my "nasty valve" had been replaced.

I had either had a stroke or a TIA, a transient ischemic attack or mini-stroke. A TIA is better because it lasts only a short while and leaves no permanent neurological deficits. In my case, by the time we got to the ER, I had recovered and might have been better off going home.

The days were filled with tests or waiting for tests. They never took place exactly when scheduled. Some of the tests were very simple, such as the neurologist asking me to touch my nose then touch his finger, or to walk a straight line down the hospital corridor. Some were elaborate and involved sophisticated machinery, such as this upcoming TEE or yesterday's MRI. I tried to do well, as I had always tried on tests in school, even when there was nothing much I could do. Except during the MRI there were moments when the technician said, "Don't swallow now," and perversely, those were the moments when I felt the greatest need to swallow, and did. The heart has its reasons.

Some people can tolerate being slid into a tube like a roast going into the oven, followed by the sensation of being buried alive to the sound of jackhammers, and some can't. I assumed I'd be in the latter group, yelling to be freed. I was offered a sedative beforehand, but it came with a paper to sign that said one possible result of the drug was death, so I chose to pass it up. As it happened, I surprised myself: I didn't mind the MRI too much. My daughter was in the room with me, and the technician, Pedro, arranged a small mirror at the end of the long tube so that I could see her and not feel totally cut off from the world of the living. This was kind of him, but he couldn't get the mirror in exactly the right position, so that I saw only a segment of her face, oddly angled, as in a Picasso painting.

After the MRI, we had to wait a long time for an orderly to wheel me back to my room; it was the week of New Year's, so the hospital was understaffed. I was more than willing to walk but that wasn't permitted. I was starving and the candy machine in the hall didn't work. We asked Pedro if he had anything around to eat. He said apologetically that all he had was a few pretzels. He gave us an enormous plastic jar with a red lid and a few pretzels way down at the bottom. We reached in, our arms in the jar practically up to our elbows. They were great pretzels—I can taste them to this day.

The preparation for the TEE is being done by a nurse with minimal English. One of the innumerable things I learned during my two five-day stays in different hospitals, one for the surgery and one for the TIA, is that the caretakers of hospital patients are nearly all immigrants. Why is this? Are immigrants particularly good at hospital care, or is it the only job they can get? We certainly should not complain about immigration because without it many of us might be dead or neglected. Not only nurses and attendants, but doctors as well (though not my all-American surgeon).

As with the angiogram, the preparation for the TEE takes a very long time, longer in fact than the test itself, and involves, among other things, the nurse spraying some foul-tasting stuff into my throat to numb it. She apologizes profusely for the taste, which I find puzzling: with a tube about to travel all the way down my esophagus to photograph the back of my heart, who gives a damn about a bad taste?

After a while the doctors arrive, a man and a woman, both very young, the man wearing a yarmulke. They barely acknowledge me lying on their table, no more than one would greet a sausage (kosher, in his case) brought in on a plate for your breakfast, in fact maybe less, and they talk to each other in low tones. Maybe they're talking about me, but then again they might equally be talking about football scores or last night's blind date or problems with their aging parents. The nurse continues to explain the procedure to me, so thoroughly that I could probably perform one myself in a pinch. Definitely a case of too much information, especially as there's a partial anesthetic so I won't be fully awake or aware in any case. They must be obeying a new law of full disclosure.

The key part of the explanation regards the tube. While the young doctors continue their murmuring, the nurse holds up her second finger and says, "We use a tube like this, about this size, to go down your esophagus with a little camera at the end." It is amazing where they can put cameras nowadays, but I reserve that line of thinking for later. I'm interested in this tube.

"You will swallow the tube," she says.

"You must be kidding." I don't actually say it, though.

Noting my consternation, the nurse says with a smile, "Are you good at swallowing big things, big pieces of steak or chunks of banana?"

"No!" It happens that I'm very bad at that sort of thing. Even large vitamins are uncomfortable to swallow. As the child of civilized parents, I was taught to chew. Moreover, ever since a teenager in our building almost choked to death on a melted cheese and sausage roll, I'm afraid of choking. Her father, seeing her turning blue, tried the Heimlich maneuver, and when that didn't work, he flipped her upside down and held her feet and shook her until the gob popped out of her throat.

But before I even deal with the prospect of swallowing a tube the diameter of the nurse's finger, I am appalled that she addresses me in the future tense, employed as the imperative. The future tense in this context is worse than the imperative itself, which would be, at the proper moment, "Swallow the tube!" If she were very polite, she might add "please." "You will swallow the tube" is a prediction. How dare she predict what I can or will do? Well, I have to be culturally sensitive, even at this stressful moment; she's obviously not expert in the nuances of English tenses. Still, she could do better. There are plenty of preferable locutions she might have used. She might even have said, "Please try to swallow the tube. But if you can't, we can use an anesthetic to get it down."

She never mentioned that option, but I learned later from my brother, who had the same procedure, that with anesthesia they can get the tube down the throats of reluctant swallowers. I should have known. If they can take out your heart for a few hours then put it back in with a little piece of horse stitched on, getting a tube down your throat must be child's play. Anyhow, I have no memory of swallowing the tube. It must have gone down one way or another, though, because I remember very clearly its coming out. The sound. I felt and heard the tube emerge from the back of my throat with a soft pop, like a cork deftly extracted from a bottle of wine.

Besides the choking incident with the Heimlich maneuver and the upside-down caper involving the sausage roll, the other thing on my mind after the nurse said, "You will swallow the tube," was a terrific movie from Colombia I'd seen not too long ago, called *Maria Full of Grace*. A young girl, very beautiful, pregnant and in desperate need of money, agrees to work as a drug mule and fly to the United States with sixty-two pellets of cocaine in her stomach. Each pellet is 4.2 centimeters long and 1.4 centimeters wide. Naturally you can't just swallow them, one, two, three. You have to learn how, rehearse. One of the most harrowing scenes in the movie is Maria being trained to swallow objects of that size. A man gives her enormous black olives to practice on, and at first she chokes and gags. But she's desperate, so eventually she learns to swallow the olives whole. Before her flight she swallows all sixty-two pellets. We see her do a few and we infer the rest. Later she has to gather them when they come out the other end—this is not shown but left to the viewer's imagination. However distasteful, it can't be as bad as swallowing them, I suppose.

I thought of that poor girl swallowing all sixty-two, while I had to swallow only one. Plus she was far from home and pregnant and moneyless. I should consider myself lucky.

Things turn out all right in the end for Maria, who delivers her cargo, has her baby and lives in an apartment in, I believe, Queens. Not so for a friend of hers on the same mission: one of the pellets bursts inside her and she dies an agonizing death.

The other movie that comes to mind, inevitably, is that old porn flick *Deep Throat*, about a woman with astonishingly ample sexual capacities, but this was the last thing I wanted to dwell on at the moment.

All during the preparation the two murmuring doctors kept fussing over some equipment on a table. I wanted them to acknowledge my presence as something more sentient than a slab of meat waiting to be carved, so I said, "Do you actually do these procedures all day long?"

"Yes," the woman answered, barely looking up.

It was on the tip of my tongue to say something about the Nazi doctors; more than the tip, the words were nearly on my lips. After all, I thought, there's a certain superficial similarity: the Nazi doctors also performed sadistic procedures all day long, though without anesthesia. Of course the crucial difference is that their goal was not to heal but to destroy. That difference is pretty crucial, no doubt about it. Enormously, infinitely crucial. But setting aside the goal, the activity itself seems not so different. I don't mean to compare myself to the victims, but merely to note again the conundrum of similar actions with widely different motives—as in the contradictions of acting on the Hippocratic oath.

But then I noticed the yarmulke. That was what restrained me from commenting. I didn't want to offend this obviously Jewish doctor, an observant Jew. Strange as it seems, there I was, a slab of meat awaiting his instruments, at his mercy, and *I* didn't want to offend *him*. Not that I feared his retaliation—I gave him more credit than that. But a remark like that would be in extremely poor taste, especially to a Jew. I was proud of my restraint. After the procedure was over, I told my husband and daughter, who were waiting outside, the little joke that I discreetly restrained, about the Nazi doctors. They were not amused. My husband said a remark like that would be in bad taste to any doctor, Jew or not, it didn't matter. I should keep such

outrageous comparisons to myself. Had I not been lying exhausted
on a gurney, he would have told me to develop some perspective, to
see things in their proper proportions. He often tells me this when
I'm in good health and of course he has a point.

All the medical people were pleased at the results of the procedure,
which showed that I hadn't had a stroke; no little pieces of grunge
matter had detached and swum to my brain. This was very good news
to me too and I was happy, sort of. But my happiness was diluted by
the imperative mood of the nurse's order—"You will swallow the
tube"—which kept echoing in my ears. I suppose I'm oversensitive
about language, and everything else.

For instance, I once tried to count how many people in the hospitals had handled my body. How many hands? I felt almost like a
prostitute, having been touched intimately by so many strangers—
and not even getting paid for it. I got up to about fifteen, unsure
whether I should count the aides who came in several times a day to
take my blood or my blood pressure. Those aren't very intimate or
intrusive procedures. But I decided to count them as well. Another
uncertainty was how many people had been in the operating room
during the surgery. I'd imagine three or four at the very least. If it took
four to do the angiogram, probably there were more in the OR. "We
reach in." Two to reach in and . . . and what? Remove the heart? Work
on it in place? Another two to attach me to the heart-lung machine
at just the right moment, before the brain is deprived of oxygen and
lapses into vegetation. After a while I lost count, couldn't keep them
all straight in my mind. Let's just say a lot of hands.

In between all these tests I would walk down the very long hall,
south to north—it covered two city blocks—until I reached the big
picture window at the north end. This second hospital was very near
my home, only a block and a half away. I'd had dealings here before:
I'd visited a neighbor with appendicitis and a friend's daughter who
had a baby; I'd telephoned the public relations office to complain
that employees arriving for the seven a.m. shift were shouting under

my window, where they parked their cars. I'd been to the emergency room a few times, nothing serious, most recently for a mysterious black-and-blue blotch on my eyelid: the doctor suspected my husband had hit me but I assured him that wasn't so. I'd brought my children to the ER for the calamities of childhood—falling off a bike and losing a piece of finger, getting a shard of glass in the foot . . .

So it was our familiar local hospital, and as I reached the north windows at the end of the corridor, I realized I could see my apartment very clearly, its southern side, living room, study, dining room and bedroom windows. I longed for wings, so that I could fly through the window and across to the comfort of my apartment. So near and so unattainable. "You are a patient."

By the end of the tests, I found my thoughts turning to leeches. In many movies set in the nineteenth century, and in the many Victorian novels I read in college and afterwards, there are scenes of sick people being treated with leeches that suck their blood. The patients lie on their stomachs, and the leeches are applied to their backs. I was always sickened by the shiny black leeches, the bloodsuckers that would gorge themselves on bad blood. Watching them in films or picturing them while reading, I would begin to shift and shrug in my chair, feeling tiny tentacles scraping at my back. I felt so sorry for the patients treated in this way, and so superior too: look how ignorant people were then, they didn't have any better treatments, they didn't know the leeches were useless. (Although I believe I read somewhere recently that leeches do have some salutary effects.)

But after all the tests I had during my second hospital stay, I changed my mind. Enough of modern technology! Bring on the leeches!

YEATS AND THE FEAR

Back at home, I gradually became aware of what I could and couldn't do. I grasped what I was now, I and my bit of horse. In a word, less: less in body and spirit—meaning muscle and mind—less in will and desire and capacity. How long this recovery would take I had no idea, and I had no idea whether I would ever retrieve the "more" I'd once had, or been. Maybe like AA veterans, I would be "in recovery" for the rest of my life.

How changed I was: my constant thought. Some lines from the Yeats poem "Easter, 1916" kept going through my mind. "All changed, changed utterly. A terrible beauty is born."

Those lines were hyperbolically inappropriate for my situation: the poem is a memorial to the Irish rebels executed after their unsuccessful Easter uprising in 1916. Yeats names them at the end, a kind of incantation: "our part / to murmur name upon name / as a mother names her child / when sleep at last has come / on limbs that had run wild." It's a frustrated, broken-hearted poem, its rhymes and three-beat lines almost like a child's verse in contrast to its content. "All changed, changed utterly."

I first read Yeats when I was a graduate student. In a seminar on the great modern writers, we read Yeats for months, everything he ever wrote, including the automatic writing that he said came to him from voices only he could hear. The teacher was dignified and lady-like in an old-fashioned way, with print dresses and white hair that looked as if she'd just come from a beauty salon, and it was unsettling to hear her discuss the more ribald passages of Joyce's *Ulysses*. There were only three students in the seminar: besides me, an Indian woman who wore wonderful outfits, not saris, but trousers and long, embroidered tunics in bright colors—I would look forward to see what she had on each Tuesday and Thursday; and a woman who was married with four children and lived right in the neighborhood. She became my close friend. She continued her studies and went on to teach at Bryn Mawr and eventually to become the head of the English Department, though she did not look or dress or comport herself in any way like our original teacher. It was in this friend's guest room that I discovered the mystery novels of Henning Mankell when I taught there years later.

Yes, I thought, changed utterly. Weaker, shakier, shrunken (I'd lost ten pounds, something I'd wanted to achieve for a long time, and now they were gone effortlessly), diminished in every way. But once again I was exaggerating mightily. What Yeats means by "changed" is not weaker or thinner but dead. "A terrible beauty" must refer to the beauty of the men's sacrifice for their ideals, for liberty, if one sees things that way. The sentiment is often invoked in wartime but I find it hard to accept. However, within the poem, I could accept it.

I was not dead for a noble cause. In fact, according to the cardiologist, I had been saved from possible death within the next couple of years. I tended to forget this, or maybe I'd never really believed it, since I hadn't had any pain or severe symptoms. I was, I am, insufficiently grateful. I'm well aware of that. On the contrary, I was willfully, ignorantly resentful. And there was nothing terribly beautiful about how I looked just now. Ten pounds less does not qualify as "a terrible beauty."

At one point I gave in to despair at my diminished self and moaned to a friend, "What did they do to me?" She was a tough sort who was discriminating with her sympathies. "What did they do to you?" she echoed curtly. "They saved your life. Have a little perspective." That again! I like those painters of the Middle Ages, before the Renaissance artists began rendering perspective from the human standpoint. Earlier, everything was flat and one-dimensional, in the same plane. I'm not ready to think in more planes than one, the most simplistic.

It occurred to me that just as future psychiatrists and psychotherapists must undergo analysis or therapy not only to know themselves, as Socrates advised, but to see how it feels from the patient's point of view, future heart surgeons, too, should undergo the procedures they will be performing. Maybe all of the resident surgeons in all of the disciplines, come to think of it: throat, lungs, liver, brain, intestines, whatever.

During my first couple of weeks at home I wasn't up to much activity, but I was determined not to sit idle. I deleted dozens of old emails from my computer, which I used in bed on a special board my daughters got me that served as a desk. Deleting emails was so dull that I couldn't do it for more than twenty minutes at a time. I recopied our address book into a fresh, empty one. The entries of the people who'd moved many times, including one of our children, are now much neater, without all the crossing out and squeezing in of the new information. In the new book, I omitted the people who had died. Most of them I'd already crossed out in the old book, but there were a few I hadn't had the heart to cross out, people I still felt close to: crossing out their names meant I accepted their deaths. Or was even indirectly complicit in them. I hadn't crossed out Rebecca or Glenda. But I omitted them from the new book. Writing them in felt too creepy: they were no longer at their old addresses or at any addresses I was aware of.

I was much visited. Visits from family and friends were pleasant, though they wore me out after about half an hour. I was visited a couple of times a week by a visiting nurse and by a physical therapist. The visiting nurse took my blood pressure, asked me questions and entered data in her laptop. The physical therapist taught me exercises to get my muscles moving again. The exercises were absurdly simple, moving a leg or an arm a few inches in one direction or another. That I, with my years of modern dance, ballet and African dance classes, my daily half hour of stretches, my workouts at the gym on machines that resembled the torture instruments I'd seen in a museum of the Spanish Inquisition in Toledo (Spain not Ohio)—that I should have to practice these infantile exercises (and find them difficult!) was mortifying.

When I told the cardiologist how tired I got when I did any exercise, he said I must push myself, to get back my stamina. Push yourself, he said firmly. If you get tired, sit down for a few minutes, have a glass of water, then get up and start again. Don't push yourself, said the physical therapist. Take it easy and never do too much. If you get tired or short of breath or your heart pounds, stop at once.

Some days I pushed and some days I didn't, but either way, those exercises and visits from the various professionals with their blood pressure kits signified that I was still a patient, even though I was in my own home and wearing my own clothes rather than the ugly white dotted gown. You are a patient, that nurse had said on the very first day. Her words had cast a spell, transformed me into a patient like a princess into a hag. What special charm could turn me back into an ordinary human being?

"Transformed utterly. A terrible beauty is born." The poetry reflected my shock. This event had never been in my life plan; I'd been told my heart was strong. I was peripherally aware of aging, but I took for granted that my strength would carry me through indefinitely. Now that belief was destroyed.

If only a terrible beauty had been born from my surgery, but that was not to be. About two months after the operation, I was over-taken by waves of fear. Not quite tsunamis, but pretty big. They swept through my body; my heart with its new valve pounded; my joints and skin felt tense; my hands trembled so that my signature looked palsied; and I had the ominous sense that something bad was about to happen. These weren't ordinary anxiety attacks, which I'd never had and which I've been told last a finite time, maybe twenty minutes. My spells were less intense, but could continue for an entire day. They were the inner ambience in which I spent my days.

I was back at work and trying as best as I could to resume the activities of my presurgical life. But now, with the fear, certain of those activities became impossible: I couldn't be with people, for one thing. The company of my fellow human beings took more composure than I could muster. Supermarkets were chaotic and bewildering. Subways were out of the question.

The anxiety that gripped and bewildered me, I learned, was a common repercussion of heart surgery. I never expected it. None of the doctors had mentioned it; it's hardly an inducement. Not that it matters much. I would still have had the surgery, and I doubt that anticipating massive anxiety would have made it any easier to bear.

Before, I'd occasionally felt what I casually called depressed, but I see now that this was a misnomer: I'd been merely discontented or out of sorts, nothing that required medical attention. These new feelings were something else. Unimagined. As if I'd been colonized by aliens bringing unknown viruses and symptoms. In fact the anesthetic I'd been under for five or six hours was an alien substance that would take quite some time to dissipate. Besides the anesthetic and the emotional trauma, there'd been that mysterious heart-lung machine that for several hours substituted for my real heart. No one seems to know exactly what effect that could have on postsurgical depression, or on anything else, for that matter.

I began each morning by looking forward to the evening, when the anxiety would ebb. Then I would carry my pillow and quilt to the living room couch and settle in with the three remotes to watch movies. I blessed Netflix. I read *War and Peace*. I wanted something that was sure to be good and would last very long. I'd read it when I was around nineteen or twenty but had forgotten most of it except that Natasha first loves Andrei and after he dies she loves Pierre. Surely there was more to it than that! *War and Peace* offered the uncanny comfort of rereading: some parts feel utterly unknown, and then as we go along, gradually a sense of familiarity begins to unfurl and blossom. We know and don't know at the same time. There's the thrill of stepping onto fresh territory, or rather territory we've visited before but which has renewed itself especially for our return visit.

I tried to explain to the doctors that I wasn't so much depressed as anxious. They said it was the same thing, anxiety, depression. I didn't see their logic but was in no condition to argue. ("Agitated depression," a doctor friend told me when I mentioned it. That little phrase made more sense.) I was again at the doctors' mercy: no longer a slab of meat in their hands but a vat of chemicals gone awry, to be treated with more chemicals, controlled substances that would counteract the uncontrolled chemicals within. They said it could last six months or more, but it would definitely go away someday. I couldn't imagine that. I couldn't remember how I used to be. Luckily I was able to walk to the drugstore to pick up the prescriptions, but waiting in line made me want to jump out of my skin.

I tried hard to think of what I was really afraid of. Everything, nothing. Everything unexpected that might happen in the next moment. Nothing I could name with certainty. I was afraid of fainting, of collapsing in the shower or walking down the street. I was afraid of facing my work. I was afraid of idleness. I was afraid when I was tired—and I was tired a lot of the time—but when I took naps I was afraid I'd never manage to get up. I was afraid of life and afraid of death. But that's all there is—what other state could I retreat to?

When I pushed my questions further, I realized I was afraid of what had already been done to my body, even though that was over and I was no longer in pain. What exactly went on in the operating room while I was unconscious? That was the experience missing from my memory, making my mind unbalanced and plagued by uncertainty. I could easily have asked doctors or looked it up, but I preferred my lurid imaginings.

LURID IMAGININGS

Forty or fifty years ago doctors didn't tell patients very much about their conditions, even when they were terminal. Doctors did not explain which procedures they resolved upon and why, or what symptoms or side effects might ensue. But over time patients began to assert their right to know, and so by now things have come full circle. Doctors tell you everything. The scientific part, that is. My cardiologist, that kindly, balding, unflappable man, told me all about how aortic valves work, how mine was not working properly—he even pointed this out on a computer rendition of my heart in action—and how the new valve would perform better. I've forgotten the details, as I always forgot science lessons right after the exams, but for a while I understood how blood is pumped through the body, and why I was finding it harder to climb subway stairs and walk up hills. I had thought that this was a symptom of aging and smoking, but no: it was my nasty valve reneging on its duty.

What intrigues me more than the biology, though, is how the surgery is carried out. The mechanical part. For instance, I have a pale pink line about six inches long going down the center of my chest, starting about two inches below my collarbone: the scar. I don't mind the scar on aesthetic grounds and I'd never dream of trying to hide it: it's not especially ugly and hardly noticeable anyway. But when I see it in the mirror, I'm reminded that it was, for a few hours, a gateway of sorts. It is the mark of a double door opening to the secret lodging of my heart. "We reach in." Welcome to my inner life, I could have said, had I been conscious when the doors opened. Some double doors open automatically and majestically, but not these. How exactly did they open?

That's just one question I might have asked the surgeon when we met, had my mind not gone blank. Now I'm teeming with questions. How do you open someone's chest, that is, create the vertical slit that allows for the double doors? It must be with a plain old hammer and saw, right? The surgeon or one of his helpers must draw a line down the center of the chest, maybe with a pencil or a Bic pen, but they can't use the hammer right away. They must have to saw along the line first. Once they've sawed and sawed, scored the chest, as it were, then the surgeon can raise the hammer high and bring it down on the sternum like Paul Bunyan swinging his mighty axe. What does it sound like? Splitting wood? Or the kind of jagged, rough sounds you hear from the back of old-style butcher shops?

So the vertical line is broken, and maybe a few ribs and other parts too. The double doors are forced open to reveal the precious beating, pumping heart in its bloody chamber.

"We reach in."

Somehow they disable the heart and keep the body alive by means of the heart-lung machine. I wouldn't know how to begin asking about this machine. Is it attached to the heart? How? And also to the lungs? How big is it? Is the heart actually removed from the body? Does "reach in" mean reach in to extract the heart, or reach in to work on it? And if they do remove it, where do they put it for the hour, or two, or three that they're working? (I hope they're wearing gloves, by the way. Of course; nowadays even supermarket clerks wear gloves.) Is it on a table? In a special dish or bowl? How far is it from my body, where it usually resides? Does it feel anything—abandoned, say? What if someone is clumsy and the heart slips out of the bowl and slides along the floor? They run to rescue it. It sounds like a children's book: catch Timmy's heart before it rolls down the hill. Is the little valve of horse sewn on with a needle and thread or attached some other way, staples, Velcro? How do they get the heart back in the chest in exactly the right position? Are the double doors of my chest open the whole time, the unaccustomed air wafting over my innards? Couldn't I catch a cold, so exposed?

I can't remember all of this, but I believe it happened, or something very like it. It still exists, on the dark side of memory. Memory has its dark side, unseen, like the dark side of the moon. Whatever is done to the body cannot be obliterated, only turned away from and hidden.

REHAB

Among the mounds of printed material the hospital sent home with me was a progressive schedule of walking. You start out with two blocks a day and gradually increase until you're up to a mile a day.

It was a very cold winter; I would bundle up to stroll along the park opposite our apartment. In the past, I used to shiver in the cold, but no longer. It must have been the bit of horse, speeding my blood on its way faster than it had flowed in years. At first my husband or a friend walked with me, but soon I walked alone. I forced myself, even when the anxiety was enveloping and I feared I might collapse along the way and never make it home. In my worst fantasies, I was picked up from the snowy ground and sent back to the hospital to start all over again. When I arrived home safely from my walks, it was with great relief, as if I had survived a perilous journey, an expedition to the North Pole.

In the midst of my "agitated depression" I began an eight-week program of cardiac rehab three mornings a week at yet another hospital. There I found some half dozen patients disporting themselves in a small gym in the basement, with the usual treadmills, stationary bikes, and weight machines. The patients changed from week to week; some graduated, newcomers arrived. The women talked in the dressing room as women tend to do. (Maybe men do too, I don't know.) Undressing together seems to promote emotional and spiritual intimacy. One woman who looked older than I but was actually younger said she cried a lot of the time. A much younger woman said she was so wretched with her husband that she had to figure out a way to leave him. "Don't make major decisions when you're so depressed," the other woman and I both advised. Just as years ago, my friends and I would remind each other not to make any decisions when we had our periods.

The last step in the dressing room was to attach the intricate color-coded patches and wires to our chests so the nurse at a computer could keep track of our heart rates, and for all I know, our thoughts and feelings too. The program was meticulously organized: each day we were given a personally tailored schedule of which machines to use, for how long, and at what rate of speed. The physical therapists were so kind and efficient as to seem supernatural. A slim, dark-haired one actually resembled Wonder Woman.

Every so often a patient would report chest pains or dizziness and would promptly be led to a wheelchair. Often that patient was sent to the emergency room, and as he or she was wheeled out, the rest of us, looking on, kept pacing on our treadmills or hoisting our weights. This felt heartless, but what could we do? It could be any of us in that wheelchair. It was best to ignore it. Leave it to the professionals.

The program worked well: the more I exercised, the stronger I got. It didn't help the fear, though. That would take a long time to simmer down, if ever. (I can see in what I've written here that some of the extreme feelings are a result of the fear. Though that doesn't mean I disown them.) Beneath the fear was the sense of waiting, which outlasted the fear. Waiting for something, though I never figured out what. Maybe for the return of my former self. My former strength, endurance, fortitude, courage.

As the weeks passed, I began to feel changes. This time I wasn't changed utterly, only in small ways. I could walk up a hill or up the subway steps without growing short of breath. I could be with a friend for the duration of a brief walk. After a while I could go to a restaurant or a movie without feeling so restless that I had to flee. I became interested in the news again, the wars and natural disasters. It was even conceivable that with patience, I would stop being a patient and repossess the "more" I had once been. Yes, I might soon be restored to life, a real life, and this real life would last longer than it would have without the surgery. And as I tentatively began to feel inhabited by this "real life"—going out to a movie, talking to people in a café, caring about my work, enjoying family get-togethers—it was very like rereading *War and Peace* after a long hiatus: stepping into territory that was familiar and fresh at the same time, territory that was being renewed precisely by my own return.

It was still hard to admit that the surgery was a good thing. Now that it was over I didn't want to think about it, good or bad. What I did think about was the horse, whom I imagined grazing in a green meadow under a blue sky. Before he gave up his heart valve, of course.

It occurs to me: is it possible that horses are killed expressly for their valves, as in the illegal traffic in human organs? On that day when I first met the surgeon, did he call a stable and order a horse's valve? I wouldn't want to be the cause of any horse's death. Be that as it may, I am the beneficiary, and I feel grateful to the horse who pumps my blood so effectively.

I never smoked those two cigarettes I brought with me the first day. When I got home I put the almost empty pack of Vantage in the bottom drawer of my night table, next to an unopened carton. They're still there, almost eight months later. Even though I probably won't smoke anymore (though you never know, I might regain my old nonchalance), I feel those two are owed to me.

This Is Where
We Came In

Every Saturday afternoon, we went to the movies, a double feature at the Carroll Theater on the corner of Utica Avenue and Crown Street in Brooklyn. Carroll Street was one block farther up the avenue, so why the theater was called the Carroll rather than the Crown I never understood.

We went sometime after lunch, whenever the mood struck and regardless of what was playing—comedy, drama, mystery, horror. Indeed, we had no idea what would be playing, unless we'd passed the Carroll a day or two before and noticed the colorful placards in their glass cases, with photos of the stars. It never occurred to us to look up the times either movie would begin: the notion of theaters making their schedules available to the viewing public was quite beyond us at the age of ten, or eleven, or twelve. Going to the movies meant drifting in somewhere in the middle of the first feature, then suspending its scenes in memory during the rest of the show—two hours or more—until the afternoon came full circle as the images began looking familiar.

We were herded into the Carroll's shadowy depths by the matron, a stocky, tubular woman dressed in a white uniform like a nurse, who seated us in the children's section, off to the side, so we wouldn't disturb the adults, of whom there were very few on a Saturday afternoon. Nonetheless the matron kept strict watch, striding up and down the aisles, hushing whisperers with stern warnings. Though we mocked her among ourselves, the matron was an object of fear because she could get us thrown out of the movie and then what would we do with the rest of our Saturday afternoon?

Our nonchalant readiness to accept whatever was in progress on the screen might sound like sweet bygone naïveté, evoking nostalgia for the simple life: no checking the time, reserving tickets, waiting in line . . . I tended to regard it as such, until I discussed it with my astute friend Alice, also from Brooklyn, who pointed out that on the contrary, starting the movie in the middle had a distinctly postmodern cast, an omen of hypertext, even: we were dealing with the given information in fragments with no context, or only a slowly clarifying context.

I thought this over and saw that Alice was right. Not only did we have to locate ourselves midplot, seeking a foothold in a zone of utter ignorance. We had to invent, by intuition, who the characters were and surmise their histories. We didn't know if the figures on the screen were friends or foes, lovers or married, and we didn't know who was bad and who was good. If someone was murdered, we didn't know if he deserved to be murdered and we should be happy, or if he was an innocent victim and we should be sorry. If characters kissed, we didn't know if it was their first kiss or their last. We didn't even know if we were close to the beginning, or in the middle, or near the end.

Far from producing unease, the condition of not knowing was thrilling. Until we gained some inkling of the goings-on, the plot was wide open, a vast expanse of potentiality, gradually narrowing as the possibilities sorted themselves out, some evaporating, others looming large, until an intentional pattern emerged.

When the movie was over, so many tantalizing questions remained: how did the whole imbroglio evolve, who was the sinister old man who turned up near the end, what treachery had taken place in that august mansion? Why was everyone bent on keeping the lovers apart? Who was the dead man everyone kept talking about? Was there anyone else we had not yet met?

It was a long time before our curiosity could be appeased. In the interval came the Disney cartoons, then a new installment of Superman—resuming whatever peril we'd left him in last week—and Movietone News, with its perennial opening footage of skiers executing stupendous leaps down the Alps, followed by highlights of current events. After the coming attractions, which we promptly forgot, we watched the second movie in the ordinary way, from beginning to end. At last, the original movie, to be summoned from memory. Now we had to reshape all the premises we'd worked so hard to formulate. So those two were not really friends at all, but rivals for the estate, pretending goodwill. So the murder we'd seen was the ultimate in a string of gruesome murders. So that man was the renegade father, that woman the long-lost daughter.

As we reassembled the plot, superimposing the actual story against the one we'd constructed from insufficient data, things began fitting together reassuringly. The movies of my childhood, a more stable, trusting era, were linear, their plots meant to be comprehended. A reliable directorial hand would guide us through the landscape. And yet the effort of reassembly, I see now, was very much like watching today's movies, so many of which are built of fragments scattered in a jumbled time frame. Arriving in the middle transformed those simple movies of the past into postmodern films. We were, in a sense, being prepared for the future, for movies that replicate, unwittingly, our experience of arriving in the middle.

The curious thing is that although I loved figuring out the movie and revising my assumptions, I don't love current movies with their short, baffling scenes, deconstructed mosaics that must be rebuilt on the spot—or more likely, in discussions afterwards, over coffee or standing on the sidewalk. There are always a few pieces I can't find a place for. Today's moviemakers are teases rather than benevolent guides; they mean to obfuscate; they set us down in the center of a labyrinthine design and abandon us. I'm quite aware that the change reflects a cultural shift: we're no longer as certain of anything as we once were, and naturally movies reflect that instability and ambiguity. But that awareness doesn't change my feelings: outside, I may have to live in chaos and bafflement, but inside the movie house, I long for an orderly world restored.

Predictably, on those Saturday afternoons, a sense of déjà vu would insinuate itself. A scene would look familiar, then another and another. We shifted restlessly in our seats, nudging each other, provoking the matron's fierce glance. Someone would murmur, I think this is where we came in.

Now and then one of us wasn't quite sure, couldn't quite recall, so we'd wait a bit until she said, Oh, right, I remember. Okay, I guess this is where we came in. Or someone else might urge, Let's just stay till the cops find him hiding in the bushes, or till the mother realizes it's her long-lost child—I want to see that again. And so we waited until everyone was satisfied and ready to leave—unless the movie was so entrancing that we stayed, by consensus, to see the second half all over again.

We didn't worry about making noise as we shuffled out; the matron's power no longer mattered. Once we hit daylight, blinking in the dazzle of late-afternoon sun, we had so much to discuss—weaving the segments together, patching them with remembered details, collaborating to achieve a design entirely congruent to the original movie meant to be seen from start to finish. Far from mere passive observers, we became moviemakers ourselves.

"I Wish I Could Say the Same"

I never witnessed the primal scene, Freud's keyhole drama in which the child spies the parents in the act. I'm not especially curious about how mine disported themselves in bed. But I have lately become curious about what it felt like for her, my mother. Granted, it's a subject I don't know much about. Whatever I write is conjecture, intimations from what I saw and heard, or didn't—what was conspicuous by its absence. I have a sense that her deepest satisfaction was in the vanity department, and the connection between vanity and sexual pleasure is even more obscure than are the facts in this case.

My father, who was such a vivid presence for me in his lifetime, has since his death been fading like a Polaroid photo going in the wrong direction, from color and definition back to milky blur. I once thought I knew him through and through, each atom; I had studied him with critical scrutiny, as daughters do. Now I'm not sure I knew anything at all except the surface. Now, unless I make a conscious effort to locate the particles of him that lodged in me, he's like someone I used to see around all the time but never knew very well—the letter carrier or the man who drove the ice-cream truck. Certain people, whether living or dead, need to be physically present in order to be fully apprehended, while others leave traces that more readily adhere. My mother remains as vivid as when I last saw her alive twenty-six years ago. I know her better now than I did then.

My mother was not prudishly silent about sex. Many mothers of her generation behaved (and looked) as though sex were not part of the basic human repertoire. For that difference my friends envied me, growing up, and it's true I didn't bear the burden of the common inhibitions. I had others, though, so I'm not sure their envy was warranted. I imagine that my childhood friends managed to get over their sexual inhibitions (people do, as a rule), but other kinds of learned fears may be more tenacious.

From remarks my mother let drop, it was clear that she and my father engaged in sex ("did it," as we used to say), that she assumed one day I would do the same, and that it was a good thing in general. The crucial words are "let drop." Sex was something to be alluded to coyly, even lewdly—a born performer, she could do a great delivery of off-color jokes, though never very gross ones. But it was not a topic for extended discussion, either entertaining or serious. I once asked her what we would do if I had a baby before marriage. "Out of wedlock," as we then said. That was a calamitous thing to have happen, or so it seemed to me. She smiled at my question; the likelihood must have appeared remote. Besides being ten years old, I was bookish and unworldly and had shown no signs of incipient promiscuity. "If you had a baby, we would take care of it," she said kindly. End of story. I was touched by her answer. I still am. Nowadays I suppose an enlightened mother would probe into the whys and wherefores of such a question, but at the time I was satisfied.

My father was the more close-mouthed on the subject. To me he never mentioned anything concerning sex, though I found out years later, with some dismay, that he was more frank with my older sister. "Sleep with him if you must," he advised her about one boyfriend, "but don't marry him." What I would have given to be addressed that way, as if I were capable of both judgment and passion! Probably he was more frank with my younger brother too, in the manner of fathers and sons, whatever that might have been. Did he think I was too intellectual ever to think about sex? Or even to require advice? In our staid little backwater, being "intellectual" and being sexual were considered mutually exclusive; it took me a while to realize that this was not true, that the contrary might often be true.

But it's not totally accurate to say he never mentioned sex. When my teenaged friend next door and her boyfriend necked ostentatiously on the front porch, offending my father's sense of propriety, discommoding him as he sat on the other side of the low brick wall reading his paper and smoking his cigar, he suggested sarcastically to my mother that the boy, who was poor, apply to the girl's father, who was rich, for "the privilege of sleeping with your daughter." Not only were the neighbors rich but they were deeply stupid, and the injustice of that combination—wealth and stupidity—drove my father wild, he himself being smart with no money. He was so pleased with his bon mot that he stomped around the house repeating it whenever provoked; my mother had all she could do to keep him from proclaiming it on the porch. I myself thought it very funny, if cruel. I found my father's verbal bursts of spleen dashingly clever. The eager couple did eventually marry. We all went to the wedding.

"I LOVE EVERY INCH . . ."

I never saw my parents in a genuine embrace. When my father left with his briefcase in the morning and returned at dinnertime he kissed whomever was in the room, including my mother, quickly but affectionately on the cheek, and during the time I was in erotic thrall to him (that didn't last long, perhaps until the age of seven or eight) I would shout "First is best," if I'd been first, "Last is best," if last, and so on. He found that cute and varied the order on purpose, just to hear it. During one phase of my erotic thralldom, when I was about four or five, I didn't like to let him out of my sight, even to go to the bathroom, and so he sometimes let me accompany him there, where he managed to urinate—I still don't know how and keep meaning to consult my husband about it—in the most discreet manner, never exposing a millimeter of flesh. He said he was watering the toilet and this satisfied me. Precocious as I was in some ways, I must have been a naïve child, or exceptionally gullible.

The closest thing to an embrace that I saw was their dancing together at family weddings, my father's rather short arms, in their suit jacket, settled firmly and formally around my mother's thick, fleshy middle. Otherwise his public displays of conjugal love took the form of mock violence. He would twist her arm behind her back, she would wince and protest in mock pain (or real pain, for all I know), and he would give an exaggerated leer. When their friends came over, he would slap her genially somewhere on her vast cushiony torso and say, "I love every inch of it." Maybe these professions were why my mother never suffered the self-loathing common to overweight women. When they went out, she dressed in tight, bright clothes and flaunted her bulk, as if she came from some distant culture where fat was prized. Paradoxically, none of this deterred her constant efforts to lose weight. She once tried some medication that did help with her weight, but it also made her chatter so incessantly that we wondered if the fifty lost pounds were worth it.

When I was very small and sometimes curled up for a nap with her, I would tell her she smelled good—talcum powder, I think; complacently, she would answer, "That's what your father says too." I regarded her naked body, which she never hesitated to show, as a kind of grotesque marvel. If I was around while she dressed, she would ask me to hook her enormous long-line bras, either "on the tight" or "on the loose" hook, depending on her state of digestion or her plans for the day: home or out. I was impressed by her nonchalance, for I myself didn't care to be seen other than fully dressed; I think this had less to do with my body per se than with my already extreme penchant for privacy, my sense of the great divide between the inner life and the outward performance.

I accepted my mother's size as a given, never having known her any other way. She was charming, well-dressed, and eminently presentable—more, she was charismatic—so I could take her anywhere, so to speak. Still, I felt that her weight made her different from other mothers. I knew for certain at a young age that I would never let my body get like hers. This resolve never lapsed. When I was close to forty, I found myself climbing up a ladder into a swimming pool behind my mother, confronting the backs of her thighs. I was appalled at their state. I wondered if anything like that could ever happen to my thighs; I resolved all over again to make sure it didn't, as far as was in my power. I also resolved never to let my children walk behind me on a pool ladder when I got old, or maybe even sooner.

"HE MANAGED TO CALL ME . . ."

I never heard my father call my mother by her name. Like her fat or his twisting her arm and leering, this was simply the way things were in our family. When I thought about it at all, it seemed a form of contempt or denial—he called everyone else by name; she called him by name—but I never stayed with the thought very long, even though I was considered a thoughtful child. I was thoughtful, but my thoughts were about what I read in books, not what was near at hand. I rarely pondered how it might make her feel, though I do now. Nor did I ever discuss the absence of the name with my sister or brother. We didn't talk much about our parents. We were spaced far apart, and as we acknowledged to one another later, we all had different parents, in a manner of speaking: my sister the young ones, I the early middle-aged, and my brother the late-middle-aged. Anyway, often children can't distinguish between what is curious and aberrant and what is not, since they get to grow up in only one household. But surely we heard our friends' parents call each other by name; in fact I remember all my friends' parents first names because in our gossip sessions we referred to them chummily that way, which wasn't the custom in public—always Mr. and Mrs.

My mother mentioned this curiosity only once, offhandedly: "He never calls me by my name," with a very slight tinge of rue, but more in the manner of noting a mildly eccentric but insignificant habit. Then, when my father was in his seventies and sick with cancer, she told me in her colorful, dramatic way, how he had been in the bathtub and suddenly gone weak and faint, felt himself sliding downwards and couldn't summon the strength to reach the faucet and turn the water off. "He could have slipped down and drowned," she said theatrically, her green eyes wide, her mellow voice almost singing (she was an amateur singer, mostly of torch songs; she had the cabaret singer's marvelous erotic knack of making every man in the room feel she was singing to him alone). "But he managed to call me. I was in the kitchen and luckily I heard him." A meaningful, almost shy glance: "I knew it must be serious, because he called me by my name. 'Sarah,' I heard him calling." She rushed in. Actually, she added, with pride in his resourcefulness, by the time she got there he'd managed to release the stopper with his foot to let some water out. So maybe he hadn't needed to break his lifelong habit after all.

"IF YOU DON'T FEED THEM ENOUGH . . ."

I also knew for certain at a very young age, after reading a sex manual in my parents' bedroom, that since there were such things as orgasms to be had, I would have them. Determination seemed needed because the author of the manual made orgasms sound dauntingly arduous for women to attain; his detailed recommendations—addressed to men—were burdened with anxiety and condescension. I already knew daily life was painful and I was intent on grabbing whatever spontaneous benefits it could offer in recompense. I might even have had an inkling that the activities the book described—however bizarre, mortifying, even disgusting—were very important, maybe even the reason why people put up so docilely with everything else.

Shortly before I was to be married, my mother gave me a gift for my "honeymoon." My husband-to-be and I didn't hold with such bourgeois concepts as engagements, trousseaux and honeymoons (we didn't see the paradox in our taking the ultimate bourgeois step of getting married) and hadn't the money or time to go away in any case. Instead we were planning a few nights in a glamorous New York hotel. As it turned out, on the second night, most unglamorously, we found ourselves having dinner at my husband's parents' house; how we allowed that to happen I can't or won't remember, but it chills me to think of it. How rife we were with paradox. There my husband became violently ill with the flu, so we ended up staying over. My in-laws put us in separate rooms so I wouldn't catch his flu. Married just two days, I wasn't bold enough to insist that we sleep together—the reason we had married to begin with—and my husband was too sick to insist on anything. I have to hope so, anyway. I crept into his room in the middle of the night as if we were having an illicit affair.

In the box my mother presented I found a pair of red harem paja-mas. The pants were tulle, very full, with elastic around the ankles. The top, also tulle, was cut like a peasant blouse, with elastic at the neck, around the short puffy sleeves, and at the midriff, which was of course left bare. They struck me as ridiculous and I said so. Did she really think, I asked, that I would ever wear something like that? She did. Surprised but undeterred, she pressed them on me—"Why not?"— and I was a trifle offended, as if she thought they might be needed, as if I alone and unadorned were not enough. I accepted the pajamas with no intention of wearing them, and I never did. I can't remember what I did with them. They were not the kind of thing you donate to the Salvation Army. Now, with years of housekeeping behind me, I realize they might have been good cleaning rags. Probably, years later, I shoved them in the dress-up basket, where my children rummaged for outlandish play-acting costumes.

The harem pajamas made me wonder what kind of notions my mother had about sex and about me. She certainly didn't own anything like them, unless she kept it under lock and key—I knew all her clothes, from the bras on out. Her clothes were on the flashy side, but never outrageous. It seemed she wished to fashion me into something that fit an abstract idea, an idea of the kind of sexual being I, or maybe any woman, should be. And this red-harem-pajama idea seemed paradoxical too, for there was a quality about my mother that I didn't especially enjoy and that I can call only "wholesome." Wholesomeness, to my mind, wiped out, like a coat of spanking white paint on a grainy old wall, most of what made life interesting, the gradual accumulation of flaws and dirt. She managed to be wholesome even when she was telling raunchy jokes. And she used humor to domesticate any unwholesome tendencies brought to her attention. When I told her something Freud had said about childhood incest, she was appalled but quickly recovered. "Sleep with my brother! I didn't even like to eat with him."

Even her sexy cabaret songs, sung so that every man in the room felt she was singing to him alone in the dark, were made ambiguous by the sunny glow of wholesomeness—suggesting that she both meant and didn't mean the words and gestures. This is how I'd seduce you if I wanted to, but of course I wouldn't dream of it. It's all just good clean fun. A kind of peek-a-boo, teasing quality. (Maybe the pajamas weren't so paradoxical after all.)

With a husband, though, the teasing would imply the opposite: I'll pretend I won't give in, but of course I will in the end. For she made it clear that wives were supposed to be on hand for pleasure and use. "If you don't feed them enough at home, they'll go out to eat," she warned me a year or so after my marriage, when I went off to visit a close friend for a few days, leaving my husband on his own. I laughed and made a weak joke about food in the freezer. Everyone knows the salient element of sexual teasing is control. Or is it the more provocative illusion of control? If the wives dole out the food yet the husbands can easily "go out to eat," then who's really running the kitchen?

I didn't think all this at the time, naturally. I suspected the reason for the pajamas was simpler and more focused: she must still judge me intellectual and innocent, in need of something to catapult me into the realm of the erotic. I felt underestimated. My sense of the erotic back then did not include red harem pajamas—she was right about that; they were a prop I thought I could do without. It wasn't that I didn't grasp the purpose of sexy lingerie, but the pajamas were so overstated as to be parody, just as her sexy singing verged on parody. She had too much sense of the comic to be a true vamp.

Later on I was sorry I hadn't had the aplomb to accept the pajamas graciously, even to understand that in some circumstances, they might play a role. They could certainly be amusing. But even had my ideas about sex embraced all manner of accoutrements, I probably wouldn't have worn red harem pajamas. Black, maybe. Yes, I might have welcomed a nice black silk nightie. Not peek-a-boo, just dark, smooth, lush and slinky. Obviously, my mother and I had widely diverging ideas about who I was to be in the conjugal bed.

"SOMETIMES IT'S IN AND OUT . . ."

When I saw my mother a few weeks after my marriage, she was curious to know how things had gone in that area. And yet from remarks she had let drop and I did not contradict, she was assuming, not unreasonably, and not with any consternation, that my husband and I had been sleeping together all those weekends I'd visited him in graduate school before our wedding. Sex before marriage was publicly taboo in the upright middle class, but as I learned later, few people were gullible enough to take that seriously. My mother wasn't, as she'd already hinted with her plans for my hypothetical baby out of wedlock. And when her thirty-year-old niece was irked by an invitation to a Saturday-night date in a motel, my mother had strongly urged her to go. Not for pleasure's sake, I know, since I witnessed the consultation—but because it might bring the man closer to a marriage proposal.

"So how was it?" she asked me, more or less. I wasn't giving any information. Fine, I said with a shrug, as if the issue were beneath consideration. My laconic mode happened to coincide with my mother's spell of talking jags, brought on by the diet pills she was taking. She'd always been a spirited talker, but the pills gave her talk a spooling, uncontrolled quality, and we would sit listening, amazed and befuddled, wondering if the skein of words would ever stop. With fifty pounds gone she seemed also to have lost some of her emphatic buoyancy, but maybe that was just age, or the dejection of eating so much less. Eventually the talk spiraled down: either she went off the pills or their effect wore off.

Meanwhile, perhaps to loosen my tongue, she said offhandedly, "Sometimes it's in and out so fast you hardly know it was there." This I received in gaping fascination, less for its graphicness than for what it might be revealing about her. Them. Was that how it was? After so long? Sometimes? Always? Rarely? Like her single mention of my father's not calling her by name, the words were uttered with no distress, a bald statement of fact. Did it pain her, make her resentful? Didn't she want or feel entitled to more than that? Or was it pleasure enough to be an object of desire? (As in, "He's always bothering me," which racier married women used to mutter, the pretended annoyance a sheer drapery for their pride, as transparent as the red harem pajamas.) If the desire she aroused erupted in such haste, maybe her vanity was all the more titillated. But hadn't she read the book, I wondered, the book I found hidden in my father's night table and which exhorted haste-prone men to recite baseball scores or whatever, indefinitely? (My father was not a baseball fan, but he was an accountant, so surely he could have found some series of figures to occupy him.) The book rated men by endurance, but maybe my mother thought speed was flattering. Things seemed at cross-purposes.

I might have pushed on for the answers to those questions, and she might have been forthcoming, particularly with the diet drugs coursing through her. But I couldn't. I felt shy. It seemed perilous: I might learn things I would regret knowing. I might have to offer some intimacies in return.

"SO WHAT'S THE TROUBLE?"

Though not as unthinkable as incest, divorce was something my mother's circle and generation almost never indulged in—only under the most egregious pressures: crime, blatant or incessant adultery, rampant alcoholism. Otherwise my mother saw little need for it. When I told her of friends who were wretched enough to get divorced, she refused to understand why. "He doesn't drink, he doesn't gamble, he doesn't run around. So what's the trouble?" That sort of throwaway aphorism might suggest she was oblivious to the infinite nuances of human relationships. She was exquisitely sensitive to those nuances. (More so than my father, one of whose favorite proverbs was "Familiarity breeds contempt.") She was articulate about them too. She just didn't consider them, however blighted, grounds for divorce.

But as with everything else on this subject, I find contradictions. Long after my parents' deaths, my sister would occasionally fill me in on events from before I was born or before I reached the age of observation, and possibly later as well, since she was my mother's confidant. They had an intimacy I could never hope to penetrate, in fact didn't want to penetrate—I could sense the price was too high. My mother would sometimes tell her she wanted to pack up and leave because she couldn't bear my father's abuse: verbal, never physical, except for the equivocal arm-twisting. For despite boasting that he loved every inch of her, he was capable of atrocious insults (familiarity indeed breeding contempt): no foul language but scathingly elegant aspersions of her intelligence, opinions and "bleeding-heart" leanings. Even at the stage when I found his cruel wit so dashing, I hated it and wondered how my mother could bear it. Since she did, I concluded she must not mind it as much as I. But of course she minded. How could she not? And of course she knew there were grounds for divorce other than drinking, gambling and running around. If she didn't claim them, it was out of fear. Love, also, or the love of being loved. All the unknowns of the intimate life. Maybe there, in the intimate life, he apologized, although that is hard to imagine. Nor can I imagine any analytical pillow talk of the contemporary "What's really bothering you?" variety. But perhaps that is my failure of imagination.

Surely out of fear, too, she didn't pursue a singing career. Fear of leaving the cozy, though wide, circle of family and friends where she was the luminescent, admired center; fear of displeasing *him*, for while he enjoyed her being the life of the party, he had to pretend to disdain it; fear of losing whatever hold she had on him, for though there was much in her to love and appreciate, it puzzles me that he, of all people, was able to appreciate it. I would have expected that rage, bravado and relentless acuity would seek their like, not their opposite. But then I would be overlooking the unfathomables of chemistry, the trite but true attraction of opposites. Also that the bedrock goodness and generosity he strove so hard to conceal could find free expression by proxy, as it were, through her own. Still the puzzle remains: not that they were both lovable in their endless contradictions, but that two such sets of contradictions could be driven to love each other.

"WHEN I'M IN YOUR ARMS . . ."

Her pride in her desirability never wavered. He fed it. After his death she confided a tribute offered when he was home from the hospital between futile operations. By then I was in my midthirties and she talked to me openly about sex, though I never reciprocated. "Here I am in bed with a beautiful woman," he said wistfully, "and I can't do a thing about it." She loved that; it made his dying easier on her. Unlike him, she didn't dwell on the pleasure she was missing, but on the desire she was inciting.

He was soon back in the unforgiving hospital bed. She sat at the bedside. I watched her lift his hand and kiss it. I felt speared by a shaft of light. I had never seen anything like this before, between them. What speared me was not her doing it, but his accepting it. He hated shows of sentiment. They embarrassed him. Maybe he would have protested—because I was there watching, I mean—had he been strong enough. Or maybe he conceded that I was finally grown-up enough to see him—and he helpless enough to be seen—in this guise, being loved, accepting love.

Not long ago, I was leafing through the books in the Little Leather Library I took when my mother died. She once told me they were a wedding gift, but she didn't say from whom. They are tiny forest-green books, dozens of them, with brown, crumbling pages, containing the classics of their time, 1925. I'd read them avidly all through my childhood, but not avidly enough, it appeared. On the title page of one, a dreadfully sentimental allegory about ardent love ripening through shared suffering into mature "Sympathy . . . the Perfect Love," I came upon an inscription: "To Baby, With Love from Jack."

So he did call her something.

Knowing him, I know he could never have said it in front of the children. Did he say it only when they were alone? Only in bed? Only when they were young, or forever? She must have liked it. Baby. His baby. A baby doll kind of woman, round, soft, compliant, fun to play with. A trope of the time, and perhaps she shaped herself to fit it by a mental equivalent of those tight girdles and long-line bras. Or else it was a shape she grew into naturally. From this vantage point, it's hard to distinguish any difference.

Yet she wasn't a simpleminded kind of baby doll. After his death, she reported—again, proudly—another of his tributes: "When I'm in your arms," he used to tell her, "I feel like nothing in the world can harm me."

"I wish I could say the same," she answered back. Or so she said.

Stone Reader

What is it about stones? Their presence in a title seems to herald a good book: witness José Saramago's *The Stone Raft*; Carol Shields's *The Stone Diaries*; Ursula Hegi's *Stones from the River*; even Harold Robbins's *A Stone for Danny Fisher*, not quite in the same league but a classic of its kind. Now, as befits the shift from books to movies as the common coin of imagination's realm, there's Mark Moskowitz's 2003 documentary film, *Stone Reader*. Apart from the producer's ambitious claim that it's about "the reading culture," *Stone Reader* shows just how far a book lover will go in pursuit of his fantasy.

Moskowitz produced TV political campaign ads as well as publicity spots for CEOs, athletes and other notables. In private life, he loves to read. Ever since he was entranced by *Harold and the Purple Crayon*, his reading habit has run rampant. He wonders, in a *New York Times* promotional piece, "What have I done with my whole life? I've spent a huge amount of time sitting around doing nothing."

Of course he knows it's not "nothing." He knows we read to generate our inner lives, and that this lifelong task becomes its own end. He harbors the secret yearnings of all dedicated readers: beyond seeking diversion or data, beyond confirmation of who we are or challenges to what we think, we long to inhabit the mind of a congenial other. When we find this rare intimacy, this affinity with a stranger's voice draped in the sheerness of language, we enjoy what James Joyce called enchantment of the heart.

Moskowitz found that enchantment in a novel called *The Stones of Summer*, by Dow Mossman. The director was a student at the University of Pennsylvania in 1972 when the book appeared to a handful of rave reviews. Moskowitz gave up after a few pages, but twenty-five years later tried reading it again and loved it. ("Unbelievably great ... Amazing.") He couldn't fathom why no other books by Mossman exist. What gives? What happened to the young writer who was hailed as the voice of a new generation? To find out, he embarks on a year-long quest for the forgotten author of the forgotten novel.

If *The Stones of Summer* is as "unbelievably great" as Moskowitz claims, and if, as he hopes, his efforts get it back into print, he will have performed a worthy deed. Nonetheless, the premise at the heart of his movie is a confusion that bears pondering. As Yeats memorably asks, how can we tell the dancer from the dance? We love the book; ergo, we love the author. We want to meet him or her (with Moskowitz's favorite books, it's always him) in the flesh—this sorcerer, this soul mate, this ghostly familiar we call the writer. From the long-ago packed appearances of Dickens and Wilde to today's ubiquitous public readings, fans flock to see the person who has given them pleasure, just as the consumers of phone sex may yearn to meet the purveyors.

But you cannot see or touch a voice. Its evanescence is what makes it endlessly alluring. The writer "in person" is no more the solitary voice whispering in our ear than the murmurer of salacious tidbits is inclined to stir us in actual life. The voice is possessed temporarily, on loan. It lends itself and we do the same, a mutual and ephemeral exchange, like love. But a love never meant to be consummated outside the pages. Reading is the consummation—a miracle, really, as the emotive powers of the book pass safely from writer to reader, renewed and available whenever we open it. The writer himself is a creature of our fantasies. Reading his or her book, we may fashion an image, which has a sort of existence, but never in the flesh of the person bearing the author's name.

Most readers simply dream on, or grow up and attend a few readings, but Moskowitz was hell-bent on grabbing hold of the ineffable. Much of his quest consists of interviews with famous and not-so-famous literary men, several of them writers who attended the University of Iowa's Writers' Workshop around the time that Mossman studied there. Except for John Seelye, who wrote a *New York Times* review, no one has heard of the book or remembers the author. A mystery. One that has Moskowitz tooling around the country dropping in on anyone with some connection with Dow, as he's called from the start: after reading his novel, the director fancies they're intimates. Lots of scenery, lots of driving (while NPR's Terry Gross talks to writers on the car radio). Seasons pass. We see the hero raking leaves in his yard; that means it's fall. It's an inept and circuitous quest, with no stone unturned. Anyone familiar with publishing could have told him that the jacket designer is unlikely to know the author's whereabouts. John Kashiwabara can't even recognize the jacket he did some thirty years ago: "I've done hundreds of books!"

What the interviews do yield is the camaraderie that springs up among book lovers, a luscious phenomenon we've all known. How fine it would be, then, to hear about the complex interaction of mind and book, the intimate geological history of evolving taste. Or about what happens when a stranger's words course through us, offering unimagined possibilities, a future cut loose from expectations. Instead we hear dozens of names dropped like code words or private jokes—books and authors Moskowitz and his new friends dote on. *A Connecticut Yankee in King Arthur's Court* is "so great, so great." *The Old Man and the Sea* is "good." Wright Morris is "fabulous."

And *The Stones of Summer*? That's what matters, after all, the enduring best of the writer distilled and transformed. We learn that it's a long novel of youthful rebellion set in the Vietnam War years; its composition was arduous, its tone is impassioned, its language lyrical and dense. What it's about is the real mystery.

Moskowitz, for his part, is mystified by the notion of the one-book author in general. He seeks answers from the late critic Leslie Fiedler, the editor Robert Gottlieb, and Mossman's agent, Carl Brandt, among others. Who can say why? Each one-book author is different. Temperament, money, the vicissitudes of private life, the changes in public taste all play a part. Publishing is notoriously unpredictable. It happens that Mossman's publisher, Bobbs-Merrill, was shortly engulfed by a corporate takeover—maybe not the only reason, or even the main one, for the book's disappearance, but it certainly didn't help.

Each case is different. It is surpassingly naïve to lump under one rubric writers like Ralph Ellison, Margaret Mitchell, Henry Roth, and Joseph Heller, to name just a few. (Why call Heller a one-book author? Or does Moskowitz mean a one-famous-book author?) "Emily Brontë died," Gottlieb notes. That explains that. By the time Frank Conroy, author of the 1965 memoir *Stop-Time* and, at the time of the interview, the Iowa Workshop's director, is asked to account for the gap in his publishing curriculum vitae, the viewer, if not the producer, grasps that the "mystery" of how a writer writes, and why, and when, with what motivations, roadblocks, spurts and aridities, will never be solved by a succession of talking heads.

Eventually Moskowitz hits pay dirt by going where he should have gone an hour and a half (in real time, over a year) earlier: to the Writers' Workshop in Iowa City, where he leafs reverently through old cartons containing early drafts of *The Stones of Summer*. The sight of a copy editor's markings makes him quiver, like a dance historian stroking Ulanova's toe shoe. The elusive writer's last known address turns out to be his childhood and present home. So a mere phone call might have saved much peregrination (but not supplied material for a film).

The person who puts Moskowitz directly in touch is the novelist William Cotter Murray, a former Iowa Workshop teacher and Dow's mentor, as Murray describes himself. In the film's most engaging scenes, the pink-faced, white-haired, beguiling Murray is overcome with delight that someone cares about his former protégé, and promptly supplies a phone number in nearby Cedar Rapids. Bingo.

And there's Dow Mossman, a seedy-looking fifty-six-year-old in a moth-eaten sweater (we get a close-up of the holes), living in a fading two-story frame house. "Welcome to the House of Usher," he quips as he leads the way to the upstairs clutter. The viewer may squirm at the gross intrusion, the existential illogic of the whole enterprise, but the modest writer is thrilled. After thirty years, a besotted fan wants to do lunch, and brings along a camera crew to boot. Mossman's quicksilver intelligence and wit—apparent from the moment he opens his mouth—make him worth the long delay. In fact, if the dancer and the dance are to be inseparable, he should have been allowed to talk for the entire 127 minutes; his tossed-off remarks on Shakespeare, Casanova and the Bible are entertaining and fertile, leaving Moskowitz somewhat out of his depth.

But no, Mossman is used as the catalyst for the director's emotion and performance. Moskowitz, not Mossman, is the star. Clearly the faux-impromptu scenes have been arranged and manipulated for optimum display. What we're invited to marvel at is not the author's gift but the director's fervor and tenacity in the service of his passion. There's actually a shot of the triumphant hunter and his bemused prey walking off into the sunset. A fantasy come to life and thence to the screen.

Moskowitz is hardly alone nowadays in conflating the book and the author, but he does so with the greatest degree of disingenuousness in the guise of humility. In this regard he's made a thorough study of Michael Moore. In spirit, the two have little in common: Moskowitz is a romantic, not a muckraker. What he's learned is stylistic. Yet despite the jeans and baseball cap, he lacks his model's disarming and genuine grubbiness; he's not funny-looking, but a smooth, confident, take-charge kind of guy. His approach to the literary men is a peculiar blend of adulation and condescension, and in the effort to sound ingenuous he comes off as merely ignorant, a six-foot Alice in the baffling Wonderland of publishing.

Moore's sly antagonism would be out of place in any event, since Moskowitz seeks out only the benign members of "the reading culture." Musing over one-book authors, he doesn't question the heads of the half-dozen media conglomerates that regulate most of what we read or see, or inquire into their demand for profits beyond what serious books can reasonably earn. He doesn't interview the chain-store owners whose strangling influence controls what gets published. How many copies of *The Stones of Summer* would Barnes & Noble order, were it reissued? The publishers would surely find out beforehand.

For publishing is not Wonderland. It is all too workaday and comprehensible. The facts that determine today's reading culture are the industry's huge and risky advances, its failure to maintain the backlist, and the pressure on editors to acquire lucrative books rather than to cultivate talent like Mossman's. (Not to mention the proliferation of e-books and the great effect they are having on the book business; Moskowitz's film was made a few years before e-books appeared and before the ascendance of Amazon.) But such facts would not make a heartwarming story. Sentimentality trumps economics. It's easier to sit by in rueful commiseration as again, the elegant Carl Brandt murmurs enigmatically about Mossman, "We do that to people in this culture."

Were stones not so propitious, a more fitting title would have been *Mark's World*. The film shows his buddies, his kids, snatches of his commercial work, his house, his car. And as in submarine movies, it's a guys-only world. The single female speaking part is allotted to the director's mother, who delivers some funny lines on her son's early reading habits. There is one walk-on role, literally: while Moskowitz takes a stroll with John Seelye, Mrs. Seelye (I presume) walks a few feet off, stealing glances at the men rapt in conversation. The absence of women is noteworthy because, unlike the submarine milieu, the reading culture is one in which they are known to participate as eagerly as men, if not more so.

Women are likewise absent from Moskowitz's bookshelves, which the camera pans lovingly. (I did spy one Virginia Woolf title.) His taste is educated and solidly mainstream except for this omission, a curious one in a devoted reader who reached adulthood in the 1970s, a time that witnessed a surge of distinguished women writers.

Moskowitz's wife refused to be in the film, he notes with amused and amusing regret: she'd only agree to show her hands and feet. The latter—actually her legs to about the knee—appear as she opens the front door to get the mail. The mail is, largely, used copies of *The Stones of Summer*, which Moskowitz has been ordering online and stockpiling. (A friend justly remarks that he's making it impossible for anyone else to read the book.)

Moskowitz says of his film, "People have told me it's the closest they've come to reading a book in a movie theater." If *Stone Reader* is like a book, it's a memoir of the self-serving variety. But of course nothing is "like" a book. For all his labors, Moskowitz cannot make reading a public act or reduce its power to chumminess. Reading is the most uncommunal activity in the world: above all, it requires and teaches solitary stillness and attentiveness. Movies exist for the eye and ear, but there is no sense organ that printed words fit like a glove. However many copies we own, the true book has no sensory existence. It is the prince hidden inside the frog. We open it, and our eyes give the kiss of regeneration. Then we embrace it, alone, without the barrier of anything tangible.

Intimacy. Anger

I stood on the sidewalk as the movers hauled my family's belongings up the cement stairs fronting our new house. They were preparing to move the piano, an old black baby grand, and this promised to be dramatic. The legs had to be unscrewed and the body brought through the front casement windows of the living room, which gave onto the porch. An audience of curious neighbors had gathered to watch. In the midst of this scene I was surrounded by a clump of girls just my size, all telling me their names at once. It was my future, come to greet me. I was three and a half years old.

By pure coincidence, six girls of about the same age lived on the same block, scattered a few houses apart, on either side of the street. To this day, I can recite each girl's address, the names of their parents, brothers, sisters, and, in a few cases, live-in grandparents, as well as the fathers' occupations: one in the diamond business on Canal Street, one shoe salesman, one podiatrist, one buildings department inspector . . . Two of the mothers were schoolteachers, and the others were housewives.

Over time we girls evolved into a family of sorts, parallel to our individual families, possibly more tightly knit than our own families. Or a pack of street children, with tacit codes and survival mechanisms, but privileged street children. After hours spent sitting on stoops, leaning on car fenders, playing ball in between the occasional traffic, we returned at night to dinners and parents and warm beds—a double life.

Like family members or packs of street kids, we might not have chosen one another if not for proximity. Circumstance, habit and the simple pack instinct kept us entwined, accumulating our group history. Together we learned what intimacy was. We invented intimacy, both its benefits and its horrors.

And in the course of our inventing that intimacy, my natural evolution took an arbitrary turn, a detour. I've wondered ever since who I would have been without the two critical events in my eighth year that caused the detour. I might even say, who I was supposed to have been. During that year something wrenched inside, a wrench of the spirit like a sudden wrench of the back that leaves you stiff and barely able to move, and even after the spasm has passed, you never again move with quite the same nonchalance, taking ease of movement for granted.

The block was part of a new Brooklyn development begun in wartime: modest two-story attached row houses called Trump Homes, built by the father of the present tycoon, a man whose ambitions or at least whose practical achievements were considerably more humble than those of his son. Before that new house, my family had lived in a two-family house about a mile away, and across the street lived my paternal grandparents in a ground-floor apartment whose tiny, shadowy rooms held a tangy smell of rotting apples, a smell I always connected afterwards with old people.

My grandparents were small and stooped and wrinkled, like shriveled apples themselves, and spoke no English. They shuffled around the apartment in their ancient cardigans drinking tea out of glasses and seemed quiet and harmless, though my mother said that in their prime they had both been forceful characters and strict disciplinarians. This must have been the source of my father's periodic shouts of "Discipline, discipline," when his children irritated him—impotent outbursts, uttered for form's sake only. Although he was a habitual shouter, rage being his first resort in moments of frustration, which were frequent, he was not a strict disciplinarian. Real discipline took more time and effort, more courage, than he had the will to give, so he left that heavy lifting to my mother.

Everyone in the family seemed to accept my father's sudden and frightening eruptions as unfortunate but incorrigible, like a limp or a stammer or a physical handicap. His tantrums left me sick with disgust, but since I couldn't see any other tangible repercussions, I must have assumed there were none. I must have thought one could behave that way with no consequences. Somehow I didn't count my disgust as a repercussion, maybe because it couldn't be seen. It festered, though, and I came to accept its festering as I would have accepted any accommodation I might have made, had my father indeed been physically disabled.

Of course there were tangible repercussions, but I didn't recognize them as such. Certain friends of my parents would disappear for months or years at a time: I suppose my father's insults at the weekly pinochle games—Moron, he would shout, or, Idiot—at some point went beyond the tolerable. After a while these friends would reappear; maybe he apologized, or my mother interceded, or they forgave him, and the whole cycle—Moron, Idiot—would start all over again.

I too had a violent temper and a very short fuse. Nature and nurture contributed. Aside from whatever incipient anger resided in the DNA, I was schooled by my father. I never used the words *moron* or *idiot*, as he did, but with my friends—the girls—I would occasionally erupt in rages and storm out of rooms. Resolving a difference reasonably was not something I had ever witnessed or imagined as a possibility. I was famous for storming out of rooms. Then I would quickly forget all about my outbursts and departures and was surprised if anyone else remembered them. My mother warned me that if I didn't control my temper, no one would want to play with me. It was, in its bluntness, an appalling thing to say to a child—hardly the sort of thing today's enlightened parents would say—but time would prove her right.

But back to the girls. Shamelessly, heedless of privacy or discretion, we told each other what went on in our houses, all of which I recall in precise detail. I knew the textures of the lives in each house, the unique, intimate tone of each family: the kinds of arguments they had, the nature of the parents' dissatisfactions with each other and with their children, the smell that met you in each doorway, the foods they ate, the sleeping arrangements. Our front doors were rarely locked. We didn't knock, just walked in and announced ourselves. A meal might be in progress. Did you eat yet? our friend would say. If not, we'd be given a plate. Or we might say, I ate already, but can I watch you? Watching each other eat was a chance to glean more intimate information, to be sifted later and added to the database.

I knew the life of that block so well that everywhere I've lived since then is measured against it and what it signified, measured mostly in terms of how far behind I've left it—a distance that can vary from day to day, not in miles but in consciousness. It's not that I think of the block with nostalgia—hardly. Rather, it is memory's default setting, permanently fixed.

I knew what phrases Lois's mother, Myrna, used when she cursed at her antic teenaged son, a Lenny Bruce precursor whom Myrna, to our delight, would sometimes chase up the stairs armed with a wooden hanger. (Among ourselves we called all the parents by their first names, which we would never have dared to do in public—Mr. and Mrs. were the custom.) Not every house was so entertaining.

Brenda's was more formal—we weren't allowed to sprawl on the puffy living-room furniture. Annette's I tended to avoid, because one of her older brothers was sullen and menacing, and the other intimidatingly handsome. Diane's house was a favorite. Her frivolous mother would join us in the living room, contributing to our gossip, advising us to put on lipstick whenever we went out: you never know who you might run into, Prince Charming might be walking down the street. Though we didn't have a term for it, we all knew there was something wrong with Cynthia's mother, who would preen in front of the mirror that covered one entire wall of their living room, smiling and chatting with her reflection. One day she disappeared and months later returned chastened, back in the kitchen and helping in her husband's shoe store a few blocks away.

Although they were not all happy families (and they were unhappy in different ways) they were what used to be called "intact," except for one, the family of my closest friend, Suzanne. Her family appeared intact, but I later learned from my mother, when she judged that I was old enough to know, that Suzanne's father, a podiatrist, lived part of the time in his secretary's apartment three blocks away, which also housed his office. He turned up at home often enough to create the semblance of an intact family, and meanwhile enjoyed this Captain's Paradise arrangement bounded by a few Brooklyn blocks. Several times Suzanne took me on visits to her father's office, and the secretary made us tuna fish sandwiches while he scraped corns in the next room.

Most of the girls had an older brother. Annette even had two, the sullen one and the handsome one. I envied them their brothers; I believed that they provided insight into the world of boys, of which I knew nothing. I longed for a brother. Of course an older one was no longer possible, but still I would watch for the first star that came out at night, and make my wish for a brother of any kind. What I had was a sister who was eleven years older—she seemed closer to my mother's generation, and in fact she and my mother were very chummy. Bright children skipped through the grades in those postwar years, so my sister began attending Brooklyn College when she was fifteen. She had to memorize poetry for her English classes and she would have me hold the book and check on her as she recited the poetry, gliding around her bedroom brushing her long chestnut hair in preparation for a date with some soldier studying under the G.I. Bill. I enjoyed all this—her glamor and her hair and the poems I memorized along with her—but it was no substitute for the longed-for brother.

The two critical events occurred when I was seven. First, after years of my wishing on stars and chicken wishbones, my mother became pregnant. Right before I was told about the impending baby, I had read an article in *The Reader's Digest* that made a great impression on me. The article said that every third child born in the world was Chinese. I told my parents that since the baby would be the third child in our family, it would be Chinese. This amused everyone no end, but I didn't understand why. My grasp of the meaning of statistics is still rather undeveloped.

My mother's pregnancy surprised everyone, not only my parents themselves but all the aunts and uncles—eight pairs of aunts and uncles on either side of the family, each pair with their several children. Later I understood that it was an unplanned pregnancy, what my mother called a change-of-life baby. She was forty-three, and since she'd had several miscarriages in the years between my sister and me, she had to stay off her feet, the doctor told her, if she wanted to keep this baby. The doctor was her sister's husband, a squat, Humpty-Dumptyish man with a low, gravelly voice and a slight foreign accent, bald-headed, as slow-moving as a tortoise. We called him The Doctor, even though he was an uncle and the other uncles had names.

The Doctor, whom we consulted about all our medical matters, always assured us that everything would be fine, but in this matter of my mother's risky pregnancy he was firm about her staying in bed. So for months my mother lay in the big double bed in the second-floor bedroom with the casement windows—directly above the living-room windows through which the piano had entered—and sometimes she would send me downstairs on errands or to fetch her food. I don't remember who did the cooking during this period of enforced repose. Perhaps my sister. It was before the age of takeout.

The second event was the Monopoly craze, which developed while my mother was lying in bed. My girlfriends and I were addicted, enthralled; we couldn't stop. We played rabidly. We knew the prices of every property, the cost of every house and hotel that could be erected on that property. The games, intricate, baroque, went on for hours, sometimes days: if we were summoned for meals or bed, we left the board with its tokens, cards and money spread out, not to be touched. The games continued in our Technicolor dreams: green houses and red hotels, yellow Community Chest and orange Chance cards, and the dark dread of landing in jail.

Like any addiction, Monopoly brought out the worst aspects of our characters: the greedy became disgracefully so, the timid shrank, and those with a passion for justice or a prosecutorial bent, such as myself, policed everyone's behavior. I watched each roll of the dice, each transaction at the bank. I never cheated, but I kept a keen eye out for cheating in others, maybe because in my heart of hearts, I longed to get something for nothing but didn't have the nerve.

The Monopoly thefts were petty: an extra fifty- or hundred-dollar bill snitched from the bank, an extra house finding its way onto some-one's property. But when I noticed, one Sunday afternoon, that my B&O Railroad had migrated to Brenda's array of property cards, I had had enough. I called her a thief and grabbed the card back. Brenda, my next-door neighbor, was a genial, not very bright and occasionally sneaky girl. She protested, I persisted and finally I stood up and kicked at the board until everyone's cards, houses, hotels and tokens were jumbled in a heap. I shoved the whole mess in Brenda's direction and stormed out.

Anger—why it erupts so fiercely, what to do with it—has always been an enigma to me. For my father, it was the immediate, unthinking response to the world's not behaving as he wished it to do, or to anything or anyone who crossed his will. But how did he get the notion that the world and the people in it would or should act in accordance with his wishes? As a Jew growing up in Russia in the early years of the century and as a twelve-year-old immigrant, he surely would have had enough experience of frustration to know what to expect of the world and maybe even what tactics might serve best in response. But character is never so rational. Maybe his outbursts were a function of temperament; that is, he was born angry, wired to lash out the instant he was displeased. Whatever the source, his pattern could be learned or inherited. I know: I was his pupil as well as his heir. And, dreadful as it feels to be in the grip of anger, I also know, as he must have known, the raw pleasure of it, the jolt of release, of freeing a vast and amorphous, pressurized hostility. Anger at the world's being the way it is.

The day after the Monopoly debacle, I saw the girls sitting on Lois's stoop across the street and went to join them as usual. When I said hello, Brenda and Suzanne, who'd been Brenda's partner in the Monopoly game, ignored me. The others greeted me, but in a muted, clumsy way. At first I was puzzled, but very soon I realized that Brenda and Suzanne were acting as if I didn't exist. When I understood this, something massive and ungraspable washed over me, like a cloud or a fog. What they call, in a snowstorm, a whiteout. I felt I had indeed turned invisible because they didn't acknowledge me. I was whited out. At the same time my whole body turned hot, blazing hot, as if I had become a flame.

The betrayal—I felt it as a betrayal though I didn't yet know the word—cut even more keenly because Brenda and Suzanne were the two girls closest to me. Brenda's bedroom and mine were adjacent, separated only by a wall. Our windows, looking out over the back yards, were some dozen feet apart; with our parents' help we'd rigged up a contraption involving a rope suspended between the two windows and a basket we guided across it, so that at bedtime we could pass things back and forth—cookies, trinkets, God knows what. As for Suzanne, far more than proximity, an affinity of the spirit drew us together. She was quick and clever and had a cynical streak that infiltrated me and which in later years I worked very hard to dig out, like an irritating splinter. But at the time I found her irreverence—towards school, rules, earnestness of any kind—immensely seductive. Maybe her cynicism came from a subliminal understanding of her father's double life, making her distrust all appearances, but this is only conjecture. Maybe skepticism and irony are bred in the bone, just as my father's anger may have been.

I didn't know what to do about the white fog and my body on fire, so I slunk away and home. Upstairs, my mother lay in bed guarding her embryo. I didn't tell her what had happened. It didn't occur to me to tell her—I was too stunned. My presence, my visibility, my displacement of space, had always been so solid that the notion that I could go unacknowledged was unthinkable. It altered a basic law of nature, like gravity or breathing. I wouldn't have known how to explain it. Besides, lying in bed had made my mother languid; she didn't appear energetic enough to take in the vastness of my humiliation, even had I found words.

For six months I remained invisible, in the white fog. I would leave my house cautiously, looking for the girls as always, but checking to see if Brenda and Suzanne were among them. A tacit routine developed. If those two were in the group, I was not to approach. If they weren't, I could join the others, who would treat me as they had before. But if Brenda or Suzanne came by, I had to slink away, because I became erased. There would have been no point in staying, since I was effectively no longer there. I became accustomed—as one becomes accustomed to a chronic pain—to being visible then suddenly turned invisible by their presence, vanishing when it was decreed that I must, like a ghost with firm and precise orders from the beyond. As far as the Monopoly games, I didn't dare show my face at them.

Reliving the story now, what strikes me with force is not so much my friends' cruelty as my own silence. I lived in this limbo of non-entity for six months and never told anyone about it. I certainly wouldn't suffer anything so patiently or diffidently today. Odd, also, that my mother didn't notice anything; maybe lying in bed so much had glazed her vision, or she was too focused on the baby gestating inside, who seemed to be taking an awfully long time to make his appearance.

But I'm judging by the habits of today, when parents oversee their children's moods, tracking every nuance and dragging it into the light for scrutiny and dissection. In that distant, blinkered time and place, parents were content—they considered their responsibilities discharged—when their children were healthy and went to school and stayed out of trouble. To acknowledge painful emotion was avoided. The war was over. Everything was fine. Only happy feelings were welcomed. In those recumbent months, my mother fended off distress as if it could infect her. Even when she was perfectly well, she was alarmed at the prospect of herself or anyone else being "upset." So had she noticed my trouble, she might still have taken the path of least resistance and waited for it to pass.

I probably played a part in keeping her ignorant. Though I was carrying this burden of isolation, a vacuum so heavy that it shattered my center, there must have been spells when I behaved like an ordinary seven-year-old. I went to school, I had my piano lessons and my books and the prospect of a new baby in the house. Some Sunday mornings, I would climb into my parents' bed to feel the bumps and bounces in my mother's stomach and to sing the song from *Carousel* where the doomed hero fantasizes about his unborn child. ("Like a tree he'll grow, with his head held high, and his feet planted firm on the ground.") My parents found this an endearing performance. They didn't suspect that I was living the life of a pariah, cast out of a family as essential to me as they and my sister and the coming baby were essential.

The baby was a boy, a brother, as I had wished. A red screaming thing. My mother was out of bed and bustling around the house as before, and my father seemed proud of having finally engendered a son in middle age, although as my brother grew up, there would also grow a lifelong tension and hostility between them. But that was way off. I wanted to hold the baby but my mother was afraid I'd drop him. She hardly let me touch him: perhaps she regarded him as more precious and vulnerable because he had cost her all those months of bed rest; she transferred the fragility of the pregnancy to the baby himself.

The baby scratched at his face and red lines appeared. The Doctor, our Humpty-Dumpty doctor, told my mother to swaddle him, wrap up his hands so he couldn't damage his face. He resembled a miniature mummy. I thought the swaddling was cruel, an unforgivable restriction of his freedom of movement. She kept him swaddled for months. He was a cranky baby and since I wasn't allowed to get near him I lost interest fairly quickly.

But while I was still excited and emboldened by the birth, I took the daring step of approaching the girls on the stoop even though Brenda and Suzanne were there. The others included me in the conversation, maybe because of the novelty of a baby in my family. One day soon after, Brenda addressed a remark to me. The other girls didn't quite gasp, but there was visible surprise, as if a ban had been lifted. As if my harsh sentence had arbitrarily come to an end. Soon I was included in the group, chatting and gossiping as if nothing had ever happened.

We never talked about any of it. I don't even recall feeling angry, afterwards. Simply relieved that my exile was over. For a while, humbled. And soon, not even that. The configuration and my place in it resumed its old shape. Brenda and I went back to sending toys and treats from one bedroom window to the other in the basket. Suzanne became my best friend again.

I've always thought of my eighth year as one of transforming agony, a turning point—literally. Something in me turned and I ended up facing the world from a different angle. I began it with a particular, if tentative, stance towards life—a confident, expectant stance—and ended it with quite another, one not intended for me, more wary, more withdrawn, as if pain might be lurking around any corner.

In time, when my father grew unaccountably—to me—antagonistic to my brother, I joined in his taunts and teasing. My sister had meanwhile gotten married and moved out, and the family divided into factions: my father and I against my mother and brother. I despised my role in this scheme but couldn't stop enacting it, so I moved away too, at seventeen. Whatever drama they had to play out, I wanted no part of. I came back only to visit.

From then on, I saw the girls sporadically. Since I was no longer living on the block, we had to make phone calls and appointments, which felt unnatural after years of unlocked doors, impromptu visits. I didn't keep up with all of them, only the two or three with whom I felt some genuine affinity. But soon even these connections frayed. When we were in our early thirties, one of them organized a reunion. We met in a restaurant like grown-ups and laughed and talked about old times, as well as about the husbands and children and jobs that had meanwhile accreted to us. But no friendships resumed after that meeting, at least for me. A few times over the years I heard of plans for more reunions that included the older brothers and some of the neighborhood boys we used to go out with; there was one in particular, a dark, morose boy I had hankered after but never managed to get near. Even though I was curious to see him—could I succeed in capturing his attention now, at this late date?—I never went.

I haven't ever been as intimate with anyone in quite that way since, yet the "girls" as they are today hold no interest for me. They interest me only as they were then. When I think of them—grown women nearing old age—I imagine them thinking of me as well, remembering everything as I remember it, each of us bearing the same encyclopedic, ineradicable history of our entwined childhoods.

Now and then I'll hear a bit of news: one moved to Florida, one is living in New Jersey; there are grown children, grandchildren. I try to picture them but all I can summon up is their childhood faces. The girls I knew ceased to exist years ago, embalmed figures in a story long over. I prefer to keep that old configuration, that rare intimacy, static, a museum piece behind glass, to study at leisure—the embodiment of my education in human relations: how close people can be and what torments such closeness makes possible.

During those months of exile, it never occurred to me that there might be help from some source—a path out of the isolation, a few judicious words spoken, even an apology on my part. None of this was in my repertoire, or in my experience. I witnessed reflexive, unthinking rage so often and it came so naturally to me that anger, even now, remains the mystery it was then, the basic features of anger, that is, which others apparently learn. To begin with, when is anger justified? No, the question only shows my ignorance. Justification isn't the proper framework for such a powerful emotion—for any powerful emotions. They're simply there, not subject to reason. But surely the expression of anger requires discretion. I wonder if, in other families, children were taught to examine anger—why they feel it, how to direct it. Whether to direct it at all or restrain it. And taught when

the targets of anger are truly deserving of it, and when these targets
are simply going about their business, which happens to contradict
or interfere with our business.

These elementary questions must sound disingenuous. Granted, as
an adult I've discovered strategies better than tantrums to use against
frustration. But I'm still uncertain which ones are appropriate, and
when and how. My ignorance reminds me of a woman I once met who
was anorexic. Please, she asked me, write down what would constitute
three normal meals; I just don't know. I found this incredible, yet her
ignorance about eating is no more peculiar than mine about anger.
Because I came upon the answers to my questions late and laboriously,
my efforts to use them feel forced and artificial, as if I were consulting
a daily diet written down by an obliging if puzzled friend.

I don't feel anger at the girls who banished me, nor do I blame
myself for being hot-tempered. The episode is too remote. Anger
dissipates; I know that much about it. At least my kind of anger:
quick, uncensored, uncontrolled, then gone like smoke, heedless of
the charred remains. I simply acknowledge the incident as something
that marked me, and the marking is what I regret.

Of course we can look back on any number of events and think,
If not for that, my life would have been different. As Diane's mother,
advising lipstick, used to say, You never know who you might run into
walking down the street. If my parents hadn't chosen that specific
house, for instance . . . If I hadn't noticed Brenda cheating, or if I'd let
it go, let her have my B&O Railroad in the interests of peace? Would
I be the happy, confident child I remember before that Monopoly
game? (If memory can be trusted.) It's quite possible I'd be eaten with
self-contempt for not speaking out, and to compensate, I might have
indulged my prosecutorial bent, becoming thoroughly obnoxious.

In any event, the marking changed the way I've behaved ever since.
I've never given free rein to my temper except, alas, with family, on
the assumption, I suppose, that blood ties can't cast you out. (Though

I saw my father's brothers and sisters—all of them congenitally enraged—not speak to each other for years at a time.) With friends I'm cautious, reluctant to give offense for fear of being banished all over again. I approach thorny subjects with what looks like patience and forbearance, even wisdom. Yet I suspect my forbearance is less virtue or wisdom than a shield against my hasty words and what they might wreak. The feeling of banishment remains, a simmering pit in the gut, something to be avoided at all costs—an avoidance as illogical, as primitive, in its way, as my mother's dread of being "upset."

Her words keep coming back to me, decades later: if you keep losing your temper, no one will want to play with you. I wish she'd never said it: it's the kind of thing that can't be dug out like a splinter, as I dug out Suzanne's cynicism. Because her prophecy came true. My mother implied, and I guess I agree, that I have something explosive inside, like a grenade, which I must keep close watch on or it will obliterate me. If I feel anger, I suppress it (as painful as suppressing urgent desire), rationalize it, hide it, try to think generous, Zen-like thoughts and wait for it to pass. It does pass, but the pressure of restraint can't help but leave bruises, permanent black-and-blue marks on the spirit.

Yes, New York, There Are Baby Pigeons

I've never found anything the least bit cute or winning about pigeons. A city without them would be fine with me. My husband was more than indifferent. He called them flying rats and marveled that a few of our neighbors actually shook out bags of food for them in the park across the street, attracting gluttonous crowds. But our hard-heartedness was recently put to the ultimate test.

We returned home from a trip to find that the six-inch south ledge of our French windows had been selected as the site of a well-built, good-sized nest. This seemed a typical example of New York City nerve—the minute you leave your apartment, by death or a lesser mode, someone else tries to take it over. My first instinct was to throw the thing out. Luckily I had more urgent tasks. The next morning it held two cream-colored eggs, slightly larger than the kind we crack for breakfast. Even I couldn't be that callous. Besides, in these eggs nestled the answer to a riddle that has long perplexed residents of a pigeon-riddled city: can baby pigeons really exist if no one ever sees them?

From that day on, the eggs were never alone. A plump, gray-black pigeon of the ubiquitous type sat on them round the clock, with only an excursion now and then, for food, we assumed. Other pigeons visited, perched on the rail like protectors. A frequent visitor was an unusual cocoa-colored bird that we fancifully decided was the father; he had a proprietary air.

We took to checking the eggs several times a day, hoping to catch the moment of hatching. Did the family know when we were there? Were they waiting for privacy? Abashed, we realized we were behaving like fond grandparents, practically tiptoeing near the window and talking in whispers so as not to startle the tots.

Whether by chance or pigeon cunning, the dramatic moment eluded us. One morning three weeks later, the eggs were gone and in their place were two quivering creatures—yes, indeed, they exist!— the size and color of baby chicks: very unpigeonlike, they were covered with a pale yellow translucent down. Could there be some mistake? We watched more curiously.

To our surprise, even alarm, the mother bird sat on the newly hatched chicks exactly as she'd sat on the eggs. We were afraid she'd crush them, but we had to assume she knew her business. She would flutter about, maybe smoothing their yellow feathers. Friends and family, including the self-assured brown bird, continued to stop by, sometimes settling in right beside the nest. Only very rarely did the mother get off the birds and take flight, always leaving them guarded by one of her cronies. Several times we caught her feeding them, mouth to mouth. It was hard not to feel slightly sentimental about it all.

To begin with, the baby birds grew slowly, but then the rate became startling. After about a week and a half they were the size of common robins, then ducklings. The yellow down grew more translucent, revealing the far less attractive pigeon colors beneath, until the young were a mottled blend of yellow and gray. When they began to stir in their nests, we imagined, anthropomorphically, that they might be tired of being sat on so relentlessly.

At two and a half weeks they were restless, shifting about and trying to stand; now they were chubby, no longer yellow at all but clearly, disappointingly, pigeons. One of them showed a distinctive brown tint, supporting our hunch that the frequent visitor was indeed their dad.

Around this time, our idyllic little foray into the ways of nature, urban-style, began to lose its romantic glow. The nest, once so impressive a design of twigs, was becoming dotted with, to be polite, guano. More and more each day.

The babies, though, were still appealing, about half the size of grown pigeons. Sitting on them, the mother was high in the nest, like a ship high in the water. At last they rose to their feet, ready to move, and to our relief, the mother got off and let them have a look at the world beyond her bottom. A few days later, we spied the adolescent birds, two-thirds of full pigeon size now, taking some first fumbling steps on the ledge, the gray-black one more daring and sure-footed than the pale brown.

This was an exciting reward for our patience. Alas, it also gave us a chance to get a better look at the nest: unsightly, with patches of white everywhere obscuring its intricate structure. It was quite distasteful to imagine the birds climbing back in after their exploratory strolls.

Under the watchful eye of the mother, the young pigeons (one completely brown by now) began to make tentative liftoffs from the ledge. But for us it was all downhill from that point. Though there was still a fresh, new allure about the pair, they were nearly full-grown and had become unmistakably what we had never much liked in the first place: pigeons. Observing them at close range was no longer the great adventure it had been in their days of smallness and cuteness.

As for the nest, it was, in a word, vile. Covered in white paste. As the attempts at flight became more successful, we grasped that the birds would soon be gone, and like thoughtless houseguests, they would not be cleaning up after themselves.

The morning we found the ledge deserted we were nostalgic, I must admit. But our feelings were mixed. The six-week romance of the life cycle was over, and our hospitality had contributed two more common urban pests to the already vast population. It had begun with the delight of finding the eggs, then the wonder of the delicate, trembling yellow creatures, and it all ended in a pile of guano. Food for thought, as it were. It was best not to probe too deeply its metaphorical allusions. Sentiment past, we got the plastic bag, put on the rubber gloves, and set to work.

Wheelchair Yoga

"The yoga teacher is coming this afternoon at two. Why don't you try it?" the physical therapist suggested to my friend Marian as he settled her back in her wheelchair. Marian had just taken ten small steps with the therapist standing in front holding her arms and an assistant standing behind, pushing the chair in case she needed to sit down in a hurry. I walked alongside.

From time immemorial, Marian had gotten up at five every morning to walk several miles before going to work. Some mornings she varied her routine by bicycling. She'd kept that up until four months ago, so it seemed preposterous that now she couldn't take a step unassisted. It was a gross error in the scheme of things and I wanted to fix it. The doctors must be overlooking some crucial glitch, I thought; if only I could locate that glitch and let them know, Marian would be restored to her former powers and could forget all about these abject baby steps.

At the suggestion of yoga, she shook her head, no.

"Why not?" I urged. "Let's do it. We can go together." We would all try to get her interested in the various activities the nursing home offered, but with little success so far. Before her illness what interested her was going to museums and plays. Concerts too, so long as the music was pre-1850. I once suggested a concert that included Mendelssohn and she drew back, eyebrows raised, as if I'd proposed something unthinkable, like bungee jumping. Most of all, she loved books. Whenever we met for dinner, we would each report on what we'd been reading and exchange titles and authors' names. She was the most dedicated reader I've ever known, except for fellow writers. But she read with more selectivity than writers, who tend to read everything at hand, even the trivial. Marian's taste was too exacting for trivia. She favored large-spirited writers who dwelled on the dismal nature of human destiny, Samuel Beckett, for instance, and she would describe their works with contagious animation, in enchantingly rich sentences, her dark eyes aglow, her voice musical and mellow, its accent unmistakably New York.

She didn't watch television, so the TV in her nursing home room was useless. Friends had brought her art books and mysteries, though she'd never been a mystery fan, but the books lay ignored in a pile on her night table. Occasionally when I visited and she fell asleep, which she did often—her head lolling to one side, her eyelids drooping closed—I would leaf through the mysteries. There was one I had started a few weeks ago about a serial killer in England; each week I turned a few more pages, but to date only two bodies had been found, somewhere in the bleak marshes.

To my surprise Marian agreed to go to the yoga class, or at least she didn't refuse.

The class was held in the dining room, where the tables and chairs had been moved aside. It was a light, bright room; one wall was all windows looking out on a parking lot and its surrounding lawn, still green in early September. One by one the residents rolled in and arranged their wheelchairs in a rough semicircle. I pulled a dining-room chair over beside Marian's wheelchair. The space in front awaited the yoga teacher.

"She's a charming girl," said a woman to Marian's left. This woman was ninety-three, she told us, and appeared to be in excellent health, rosy-cheeked and sprightly. She had been a buyer for Lord & Taylor and was originally from Virginia but had lost most of her accent, she said, though in this last she was mistaken. "Charming," she repeated. "Always smiling and cheerful. We're lucky to have her." She leaned over to nudge Marian. "You should come every week." Marian proffered her dazzling smile—a quick flash of teeth, her big dark eyes gleaming so that they looked even larger. The smile and the eyes were all that remained intact while the rest of her was falling away. The smile, now as in her days of health, a mere few months ago, was like a net of sunlight flung over you.

When she was first brought to the nursing home, Marian had said she didn't feel she belonged among her fellow residents. They were "they," the old or sick or moribund or forgotten. She was "I." There was no "we." I wondered whether agreeing to take the yoga class meant she now accepted being one of the group, or whether her attendance was only provisional, like mine.

The teacher sailed into the room, all smiles, as predicted. She was slim, young, and blonde, with curly hair and milky skin. "And how are you all this afternoon?" she asked, gazing intently at the class of about twenty-five people, four of them men. All wore nondescript clothing—bland-colored slacks and shirts, faded cardigans, a few of the men in checks and plaids—except for the former buyer for Lord & Taylor, who was dressed and made up as if for a ladies' lunch. Still, everyone was neatly turned out, a credit to the staff of this humane place on a green hill in a suburb that was also home to a prison, so that most of the people who got off the train and shared the waiting taxis were going to visit either the prison or the nursing home.

Marian was definitely not a yoga type. She was skeptical of everything the least bit faddish or ameliorative. In the same vein, she distrusted any kind of zealotry or political enthusiasm. I think in her youth she had had political enthusiasm but had been disillusioned, and typically, once something disappointed her, she wanted no further part of it. She erased it from her personal landscape. I imagined that the skepticism came from her training in the Freudian tradition, for she was a psychiatric social worker. Vanity, all is vanity, or sublimation, or something of the sort, though I couldn't mount a logical argument on that score. It wasn't that she distrusted enthusiasm itself: she had it in abundance, but she reserved it for weighty, durable goods like the works of Thomas Mann. Samuel Beckett aside, she had a penchant for the Germanic, the heavy, the somber, the perverse, and when describing such books with her glowing animation, she would make them seem dazzlingly aglow as well, though they weren't. She had no interest in political or social themes, and if I tried to interpolate them, she would listen politely, then say, "Yes, okay, but . . . ," and return to her preoccupation with the intricacies of human behavior and the generally hopeless nature of human destiny, all presented with such vast enthusiasm that each book sounded like her private discovery, as if no one had ever read it before. The appeal of her enthusiasm was its purity, and by purity I mean it was untinged by the professional writer's focus on craft—how it was done rather than what was done. I had enough of the former from other writers. Marian read for the savory pleasure the books gave, and that pleasure was in perpetually broadening and deepening her understanding of the dismal human condition.

I was not a yoga type either, but for different reasons. I had taken three or four yoga classes in the past, at wide intervals, and would come away contented yet not sufficiently motivated to return. After a while I'd try again, thinking vaguely that perhaps I hadn't been in touch with my yoga vibes (thinking about yoga generates this sort of language). In fact, I found yoga too static. I preferred classes where you jumped around, modern dance or Afro-Caribbean dance, where the drummers kept up a steady uproarious beat that inspired ever greater efforts of will and exertion. Yoga classes, in my limited experience, transpired either in silence or else accompanied by a kind of soporific, underwater, insipid music, which was precisely what I now heard emanating from the back of the dining room.

We began as usual with deep breathing. We relaxed all the parts of our bodies, starting from the feet. Then we proceeded to arm movements. Up, down. Up, down. To the side and down. Five or six of the students appeared very relaxed, indeed asleep or otherwise unconscious. One man who'd started out peppy had already nodded off. Others were attempting the arm movements but not doing them properly. The woman at the end of our row, for example: when the teacher said *up*, she moved her arms to the side, and vice versa, which irritated me. I wanted to fix her.

Marian was doing better than I'd expected. On previous visits, she'd told me she couldn't get her legs to move, but now she was bending her knees, flexing her ankles, moving her feet in small circles, whatever the teacher said. She even wanted to lower the footrests on the wheelchair so she could put her feet on the floor, as some of the postures required, so together we figured out how to do that. Wheelchairs are unnervingly complicated.

I, needless to say, was the best in the class, far more accurate and vigorous than the others. I mention this not to boast, but because it was a new and gratifying experience for me—doing so well in a movement class, that is. I've taken many such classes over the years, not only modern dance and Afro-Caribbean, but ballet and jazz. Never before had I been anywhere near the top of the class. I usually brought up the rear. My timing was excellent, I could stay unfailingly on the beat, but I was not good at picking up the patterns, especially when they got complex, which they invariably did as the class progressed.

Amid the wheelchairs in the nursing home, however, I excelled. I was pleased with this unexpected bonus added to my visit. I usually came away feeling discouraged and impotent because there was nothing I could do to stop the inexorable, nothing I could fix. I couldn't locate the glitch. I could only watch. Once I watched as Marian was being weighed. The scale was curious: a large, elaborate contraption that included a chair. An attendant helped her get from her wheelchair to the scale chair by bringing the two very close together and then maneuvering so that she wasn't on her feet for more than a second or two. She weighed ninety-two pounds. The next week she told me she had lost four pounds.

Even for a person who craved thinness, this was too thin. Marian was built small, of average weight or less, but was always dieting, and the diet, as I'd observed during our many dinners out, consisted of roast chicken and green salad. No matter what type of restaurant, she always managed to find roast chicken on the menu. Sometimes I would try to tempt her by reading aloud the descriptions of succulent dishes, but she would only flash her dazzling smile and, with a tinge of irony, say firmly, no. She would leave half her portion of roast chicken, sometimes with a bit of potato alongside, and ask the waiter to wrap it up. "That will be for tomorrow."

The yoga teacher kept saying, "Good, good, that's fine, that's right," but the class didn't look fine to me. They barely raised their legs from the floor. Their arms were limp, their posture sagging. The woman at the end of our row persisted in her willful disregard of the instructions, bending when she should be straightening, raising when she should be lowering, and so on. More people had fallen asleep or showed the signs of sleep. Others were awake but not participating, just occupying space. I wanted to stand up and declare that as long as they were here they might as well take part; I believed in that as a general principle of life. But of course I restrained myself.

The teacher didn't seem to mind their nonparticipation, though. The teacher was happy to accept any halfhearted or faulty effort, even no effort at all. She had no standards, or perhaps had abandoned her standards when it came to wheelchair yoga. Unlike me, she had no longing to fix anything. She was an accepter. "Good, that's fine, that's right."

Marian, on the contrary, performed valiantly, especially given that she was dying of cancer of indeterminate origins, with fluid on the brain that made her constantly dizzy and nauseated; also, she could hardly swallow any longer. An aide had just brought her some grainy mush in a tiny paper cup: it was easier to swallow something viscous rather than liquid. Marian told her to set it aside, she'd take it later. Good, I thought. What was the urgency, after all? Had it been a martini, maybe she would have paused for a sip. At dinner, her one indulgence had been an extra dry martini, which she would order with great specificity—very dry, very cold. All her sensuality was concentrated in that martini, which she sipped slowly, making it last. But martinis were not on the menu here, though roast chicken and salad probably were.

I used to tease her about the roast chicken she carried home in a plastic bag. "But what about the rest of the week? Always roast chicken?" To entertain me, she gave a catalogue of what she ate for lunch and dinner every day, and this catalogue resembled a comic monologue out of a Beckett play. Besides the heated-up dinners of leftover restaurant chicken, there were the lunches. Every Sunday night, she explained, she made two kinds of salad, tuna and chopped herring, and then made five sandwiches which she lined up in the refrigerator, removing one each day, alternating between the tuna and the chopped herring. "But don't they get soggy, all week in the fridge?" "Not at all," she said. They kept fine.

I was intrigued by all her habits, not just the dietary; they were, to put it mildly, routinized. Besides getting up at five in the morning to walk or bike, on Tuesday mornings she got up even earlier and cleaned her whole apartment. On another morning, I forget which, she did her week's shopping. When I asked if it didn't get dull, knowing exactly what she would be doing when, she said no, that was exactly what she liked. Weekdays, after work, she would read, then go to bed very early, usually by eight o'clock. Sometimes when we'd been out to dinner on a Friday or Saturday, she would drive me home—she zipped around the city in a small, dark Toyota—and I'd invite her up to my place for a while. "No!" with a look of horror. "It's already very late for me." This was at about nine or nine-thirty. Then, grinning at her own eccentricities, she would rev up the little Toyota and charge off into the night.

Every few years she replaced the Toyota, but the new car was always so much like the old one that I couldn't tell when she'd made a change. She had formidable luck finding parking spaces on the streets of Manhattan. This, I was convinced, was because she was cavalierly optimistic about finding them. Those who expect success tend to find it, I've noticed. I envied the bravado with which she handled the car, but maybe bravado is too strong a word—there was nothing prideful about it, simply the same thoughtless ease I also envied in the better students in my dance classes. What a mordant twist, I thought, that after being so adept on wheels, on her bike, in her car, she should be confined to a wheelchair.

I had to admire the yoga teacher's ingenuity. Notwithstanding the wheelchairs, she devised movements that exercised every joint, even the hips. Still, it bothered me no end—it offended me aesthetically— that she didn't correct the class's flawed performance. Of course I knew this wasn't a performance; it was a class. But I tend to regard everything done in public as a performance, and the fact that these students were old or sick or moribund did not alter this tendency. Had they no pride? It was all I could do to stay in my chair and not go around fixing them. I wanted so much to fix them and make them do it right, the way it should be done. But I could only try to make up for the shortcomings of their performance by my own excellent one.

The class was scheduled to last an hour. About fifteen minutes before the end, when we had moved every movable part, the teacher had us close our eyes and again relax from the feet on up. To relieve the boredom, I peeked. All eyes were obediently closed. But was it true yogic relaxation or ordinary sleep? Could the yoga teacher tell the difference, and did she care?

At last, breaking the silence, she announced that she would go around to each person in turn to give a back and shoulder massage. I wondered if she would come to me, if I was considered part of the class by virtue of my earnest participation. I peeked again. She was standing behind one of the men and gently massaging his shoulders. I closed my eyes. I might as well relax along with the others: I had the train trip ahead and was planning to go to the gym once I got back to the city.

She didn't massage me. I was both disappointed and relieved. Disappointed because I felt I had earned the right to be considered part of the class. Relieved because I was spared the sense of awkwardness, even of bad faith, had I received her massage—as if to merit it I ought to be old or sick or starved for a human touch. Marian must have had a massage while my eyes were closed, even though she was not starved for a human touch, not one of those who languish alone in their last days. But everyone with a terminal illness is alone. This I learned from my watching, and Marian surely knew; she didn't need Samuel Beckett to teach her that.

Suddenly I was roused by applause and thank-yous. The wheelchairs were rolling; people were leaving the class. I must have dozed off.

Marian and I agreed that we had had a good time. But she was worn out from the effort. She swallowed a bit of the stuff the aide had left and I wheeled her back to her room, where she fell promptly asleep. I read a few more pages of the mystery; no further bodies were found. Soon it was time for me to go. We hadn't had much chance to talk, and I missed that. Her conversation was sustaining. Early on in her illness she had seemed confused—maybe it was the medication or the fluid on her brain—but lately, to my relief, she had recovered her lucidity; her analytic bent was resurgent. She was grimly articulate about how she felt. "Terrible," she would say each time I asked. "How are you?" seemed a foolish question at this point, but it's hard to break the habit. Terrible, and she would launch into a vividly detailed account of being helpless and sick and facing death. Though she never spoke about death itself, only of her illness. What she feared, she said, was what further sufferings and limitations and indignities it would force upon her. That unknown frightened her more than the unknown of death.

But that was only a small part of what we talked about. Often she would ask if I'd seen any good movies or read any good books since my last visit; she wanted to hear the plots. The week before, I'd told her about a droll French film called *Intimate Strangers*: a woman walks into a lawyer's office thinking he's a psychiatrist and begins to unburden herself, and soon a close relation develops between the two, based on this misconception. That was the sort of story Marian loved, and she listened with some of the old radiance in her eyes. *Intimate Strangers* was the last movie I got to tell her about. I had also seen *Spider-Man*, but when I mentioned it, she laughed as though it were beneath consideration, which incidentally I thought too.

I couldn't make it to the nursing home the next Wednesday so I called a good friend of Marian's and told her, "In case you're there on Wednesday, go to the yoga class at two. She really liked it. So did I." But as it turned out, Marian wasn't strong enough to take the yoga class the following Wednesday or any of the succeeding Wednesdays. Ours was her first and last yoga class, and if she hadn't been so sleepy she would have liked talking about it afterwards. No wonder, then, that I'm writing this with her in mind. She of all people would have appreciated what I have chosen to include and exclude. She wouldn't have been put off by how I describe the students in the class, and she would have understood my discontent with the yoga teacher, though she wouldn't have shared it. She would have been accepting. She would have nodded in her wry way and offered a smile of amused understanding, the smile that hung on when nearly everything else was gone.

It happened that I took another yoga class a few weeks later, with ordinary ambulatory students, and as usual in those circumstances, my performance was mediocre. I could only excel at wheelchair yoga, amid the moribund, and I finally accepted that, along with all the rest.

Thriving on Hardship

I met Hayden Carruth one summer in the mid-1980s. We were teaching at a writers' conference at a university in New York State, the kind of conference where lots of workshops and heady talk about literature are crammed into a few days, and teachers are quickly exhausted, while students drift close by, awaiting the magical words, the revelatory secrets, that might be uttered at any moment. Hayden and I were both feeling discontented and estranged from what was going on around us—I jogged through a nearby cemetery each morning for distraction; I don't know what he did—and our friendship germinated from that shared discontent. Fruitful grounds for friendship, as it turned out. We began corresponding—long, detailed letters that continued for years, punctuated by occasional phone calls and visits. Drawers full of letters by this time; sometimes he enclosed new poems. After a while the poems appeared in his books—a dozen or so books since I first met him (and almost a dozen before that)—but when I want to reread them I look for the manuscripts because they feel fresher and more intimate and were addressed to me, even if only on their envelopes.

What I relish particularly in Hayden's poems is how they revel in raw misery. At every stage of life his laments, whether raging, witty or somber, are so succulent, so vivid, so thoroughly and actively engaged in the wretchedness du jour. "Yes, William," he writes to an imaginary friend,

> I've been
> God knows, a complainer. It was
> either that or silence. Poets
> are deprived of stoicism.

They are deprived of stoicism because they must tell the truth as they feel it, emotional and intellectual accuracy, to Hayden, being a moral imperative, from the proper placement of a comma to the proper exposition of current political reality. ("Let us speak plainly," he addresses the president in "Complaint and Petition": You are / deviously and corruptly manipulating / events in order to create war.")

Sorrow and travail attended him faithfully throughout his life, and in return for their companionship, he portrayed them with the attentive, obsessive scrutiny that memoirists use for their close friends and relations. In midlife he reports,

> I am fifty-three going on fifty-four,
> a rotten time of life. My end-of-winter clothes
> are threadbare, my boots cracked, and how
> astonishing to see
>
> my back, like that figure in Rembrandt's drawing,
> bent.

But what time of life has not its own variety of rottenness? "The purposelessness of it all, of existence as such," he tells us in *Reluctantly*, a collection of autobiographical essays, "had struck me at so early an age that I have no idea when it happened or how." He suffered inter-mittently from mental disorders that had him in and out of institu-tions, as well as from alcoholism and the more commonplace sorts of anguish. Afterwards, he was devastatingly bitter or amusing and gave us some of his best "loquacious stammering" on the humiliations of old age.

And yet this is the same poet who, in his rotten fifties, writes, "I can't / help it, I have so loved / this world." Who, decades later, having rediscovered love—genuine this time, he assures us and himself—exults in "the stupendousness / of life." Who at age seventy-five writes a poem of gratitude:

> My prayers have been answered, if they were prayers.
> I live.
> . . .
> I prayed. Then on paper I wrote
> Some of the words I said, which are these poems.

Even after his suicide attempt, recounted in *Reluctantly*, a rare hap-piness came over him as he returned from the "blackness," death's entryway, a place he found "not at all uncomfortable but quite the contrary: it was happy . . . in the sense of *blissful*, a replete contented-ness. It was a state of mind I had never experienced before . . . but it was present in my mind clearly and strongly when I first came to. And it has been present ever since, it has become part of my being . . . I was high on life, my recovered life."

So he is a poet of contradiction, and a contradiction entirely natu-ral and universal: despair coupled with the will to continue, disgust at what the world offers coupled with curiosity and hope about what it will turn up next, even when he had been at the point of saying fare-well. The capacity to feel and acknowledge extremes of pain evidently coexists with—or engenders—the capacity for extremes of joy as well.

At the close of the conference where we met, there was a big dinner for students and faculty. Hayden and I sat together, and next to us sat a young man who wrote fiction (and very shortly afterwards died of AIDS). He asked us what percentage of human experience could be expressed in language. Ninety percent, I answered thoughtlessly. Ten percent, said Hayden, grimly. I have always remembered this. When I read his poems I think of the ninety percent submerged—all that ineffability, intractable yet somehow evoked by the fraction on the page, like a scent, a vapor or effluvia rising from a few grains of a potent spice.

Over and over in the voluminous work of this self-proclaimed "language-driven" poet, for whom "appearance is nothing until it has been spoken and written," comes the notion of the failure of words: "Insurmountable the uselessness of words." In "On Being Asked to Write a Poem against the War in Vietnam," he recalls earlier wars he's lived through and earlier poems deploring them:

> and not one
> breath was restored
> to one
>
> shattered throat
> mans womans or childs
> not one not
>
> one
> but death went on and on . . .

Besides the futility of words, he mourns their incapacity to render what he so desperately wants rendered. That doesn't deter him, though, from attempting the most recalcitrant and necessary subjects, those least likely to yield to language, for example, the death of his mother and the death of his daughter. Near the opening of the poem about the latter, "Dearest M—," a "gush of words, this surging elegy," he frankly admits defeat:

> The immensity of what should be said
> > defeats me. Language
> like a dismasted hulk at sea is overwhelmed
> > and founders.

That said, he goes on to conjure up his daughter Martha from the instant of her birth through her years of youth and beauty, her loves and her painting, her triumphs and the indignities of her illness. Language may be abysmally inadequate, but it is the single thing he securely possesses and inhabits, and so he deploys it not merely with technical skill but with valor: he wrestles with the inaccessible and wins, as far as that is possible.

The pain he feels at the death of his mother is of a different sort. The agony is less pure, less unitary, more tangled in a skein of ancient griefs and grievances, moments of ambiguous intimacy and gaps of misunderstanding. His mother suffered terribly for three years, and his elegy, "Mother," does not neglect the physical details. But what galls him most is her loss of language, the mystery of what she might still know, what form of consciousness might remain in her "half-dead mind." "You in your language broken, stammering, whole aggregates of once-luminous words blown out." Above all, "Was your damaged brain the same as a damaged soul?" This is the mystery whose sting does not relent, the essential riddle whose answer will never come:

> As if you were an animal somehow granted the power to
> > know but not to think,

Or as if you were a philosopher suddenly deprived of every
    faculty except
Original fear and pathos. I cannot surmise a state of being
    more inconsonant
With human consciousness.

I like that "surmise," that "inconsonant." In the midst of passionate grief, the poet's indefatigable intellect goes chugging on, prying
at the enigma at the center of his own life and work. How much of
what we know is in our words? What do we know beyond words, and
how can we know or say it? How much can a mind without words
comprehend? And finally, what is there to know? He has brooded on
this always: witness an earlier poem, "Cowshed Blues":

    in the mystery of the word

    is a force
    contained but not expressed
    spoken and unexplained

    for meaning falls away
    as the stars in their spirals
    fall from the void of creation

Nevertheless, he has been the most prolific and articulate of contemporary poets; in the face of his own pessimism, he never stops
returning to language, the unreliable ally that will not abandon him,
that he can count on for ten percent of what he needs.

Critics have noted the variety of Hayden Carruth's work, in style,
form, breadth and range of themes—love, rural life, war, jazz, the
idea of community and its assault by the current "sanctification of
avarice" are only a few. The work that draws me most, regardless of
subject, is that of the last two decades, perhaps because it was written

while I knew him. But more, I think, because it has the stamp and tone of ripened experience: a certain ease and confident looseness, a relaxation even when the poems are in a formal mode, as if the rigors of poetry have been so well absorbed that the poet writes effortlessly. Rigor is already part of his musculature and neural pathways; none of the usual barriers or anxieties interfere with the direct transference of emotion and thought into syllable and rhythm. Or at least they don't seem to: Hayden compared the writing of poetry, on his dark days, to squeezing hardened glue from a tube, though the reader would never know it. Certainly not in "Agenda at 74," a funny catalogue of an old man's fragmented day spent in trivial activities (except maybe for "write President," "write congressmen," and "write letter to the editor") linked by the repetition of "tap barometer," a compulsive, futile checking to see what the weather—no doubt inner as well as cosmic—has in store.

Also notably un-glue-like is the limpid unfurling of words in "A Few Dilapidated Arias," the last group of poems from his latest collection, *Toward the Distant Islands*, spanning work from 1959 to 2005. Here, with deceptive casualness, the poet unburdens his mind—as active as his physical abilities are curtailed—after a fallow spell. The poems have the nonchalance of cultivated skill associated with the "late style" of the great poets and composers, though not their frequently imputed serenity or resignation. They open with a dazzling image and move from strength to strength like a Brahms symphony, now thundering, now muted, now wistful:

> And thus the morning has descended. Slowly like
> a tremulous lady down the great stairs of the East.
> What I notice is language pressing in my mind,
> surprising me, as in those times when I made poems
> like sweet tarts cooling on the windowsill of a
> studio in the woods . . .

So let the sentences unfold again, like a measuring rule
jerked into angled shapes that nevertheless trace
the line onward toward resolution. Let them be
a little sonorous, but only a little.

Even earlier, he was bemoaning his own "slipping." "Song: Luxury,"
written in his mere sixties, declares:

> Even to think
> of installing an air-conditioner
> in his car is
> to the old man a
> shame and hurt,
> who throve on hardship.

"Who throve on hardship" becomes the pungent closing refrain of
each of the four stanzas; it echoes the life of arduous labor described
in *Reluctantly*, when he lived with his wife and son in rural Vermont
and did physical work all day, for himself and his neighbors, then
various sorts of editorial work for hire all night, for extra money, then
wrote poems in what time remained. In that essay he urges hardship
on young writers, especially graduate students poised to enter the
relative ease of the academic world. "If your life is easy, your writing will be slack and purposeless . . . You need difficulty, you need
necessity. And it isn't a paradox that you can choose necessity, can
actually create necessity, if you seek the right objectives; not the great
metaphysical necessity, but your own personal necessity; and it will
be no less inexorable because you have chosen it. Once you are in it,
your writing will be in it too." This in opposition to young writers'
customary view that the academic life will leave them "time to write."
Time, yes, but what intensity? Write out of what urgency, if not the
press of practical necessity against passionate desire?

The most poignant and scrupulous poem about old age is "In the Long Hall," from the 1996 collection *Scrambled Eggs & Whiskey*, an extended metaphor for writing poetry as well as watching one's life ravel and unravel with the passage of time:

> On his knees he was weaving a tapestry
> which was unraveling behind him. At first
> he didn't mind it; the work was flawed,
> loose ends, broken threads, a pattern
> he could not control; but as his skill
> improved he began to resent the way
> his tapestry was undoing itself.
> He resolved not to look back
> but to keep going ahead, as he did
> successfully for a long time. Still
> later, however, he began to notice
> that the part of the tapestry in front
> of him was unraveling too; threads
> he had just knotted became loose.
> He tied them again. But before long
> he could not keep up, his hands
> were too slow, his fingers too weak.
> The unraveling in front pushed
> him toward the unraveling in back
> until he found himself isolated
> on a small part of the tapestry whose
> pattern he could not see because
> it was beneath his own body. He spun
> this way and that. He worked as fast as
> he could with trembling fingers
> in futility, in frenzy, in despair.

But to offset the futility and despair the aged artist feels on contemplating his work, Hayden's late poems introduce an unexpected theme: romantic love. Not new, for he has often written of love before, in *The Sleeping Beauty* and elsewhere, but now refreshed and revivified. Love has come once more, surprising him, eliciting a self that is new as well. He welcomes love with unabashed gratitude and wonderment, in a series of sonnets from the late 1980s, some colloquial and others highly formal, evoking Wyatt and Donne. "More and more I believe the age demands / incertitude," and of course he means his own advanced age as well as the age in which we all uneasily reside.

> I am no one. Yet your hands
> touching, word-like, can make a person. Who
> is this strange new myself? Woman, do we know
> the I of love that you in love bestow?

Inevitably, poems written in old age will be about approaching death, but few treat death in the same breath as erotic love, as Hayden does in "Testament," from *Scrambled Eggs & Whiskey*. In fluid language and easeful music, he offers the conventional image of the hourglass to represent life seeping away, then puts that image to entirely original and startling use:

> Yet not only our lives drift down. The stuff
> of ego with which we began, the mass
> in the upper chamber, filters away
> as love accumulates below. Now
> I am almost entirely love.

What can he leave his wife, he wonders, as "the sands / in the upper glass grow few"?

All our embracings?
I know millions of these will be still
unspent when the last grain of sand
falls with its whisper, its inconsequence
on the mountain of my love below.

Words may be maddeningly inadequate, and yet the lover's hands
that "make a person" are "word-like." Words can make a person; they
have certainly made this poet. And he in turn has made the poems
that are "a gift, a bestowal / . . . what instinct is for animals, a continu-
ing and chiefly unthought corroboration of essence." This is from
"The Impossible Indispensability of the Ars Poetica," another love
poem, where he muses on what a poem is and is not. In the end, it is
the elusive, not the articulated, aspect of poetry that enthralls him:

it has almost the quality of disappearance
In its cage of visibility. It disperses among the words. It is a
fluidity, a vapor, of love.

The negative, disappearing quality of poetry returns us to the ineffable, Hayden Carruth's true habitation, the vast tracts of consciousness that words cannot begin to clarify. This fluidity, this vapor of
love, he hovers over in the extraordinary "Words in a Certain Appropriate Mode," a poem that in its strategy is as evanescent as trying to
catch a wisp of smoke in the hand, and yet precise in its limning of
the effort. It is about an indefinable locale in consciousness, the nothingness within that contains the fullness of the inexpressible world,
perhaps like the blackness of the near-death moment from which he
emerged so strangely happy:

In the everywhere that is nowhere
Neither the inside nor the outside

...

Where one is neither alone
Nor not alone, where cognition seeps
Jactatively away like the falling tide
If there were a tide, and what is left
Is nothing, or is the everything that keeps
Its undifferentiated unreality...
Where there is neither breath nor air
The place without locality, the locality
With neither extension nor intention
But there in the weightless fall

...

Without leaf or star or water or stone
Without light, without sound
                    anywhere, anywhere...

Heinrich Mann's
Man of Straw

American awareness of Heinrich Mann has not improved much since
the day he reached New York Harbor on a Greek ship in 1940, following a wartime cloak-and-dagger escape to Lisbon through the goat
paths of the Pyrenees. He came with his wife and nephew, to join his
younger brother, Thomas, in exile. Mann's biographer, Nigel Hamil-
ton, in *The Brothers Mann*, stresses the irony of the *New York Times*
report of the event: "Golo Mann, celebrated German author (he had
yet to write a book!) and son of the famous novelist Thomas Mann,
had arrived on American soil, 'accompanied by his uncle Heinrich.'"
(The succeeding quotes from Mann's letters are also from this excellent biography.)

Uncle Heinrich, at that point, had written some dozen novels
as well as novellas, short stories, plays and political essays; he was
a major German man of letters, well traveled, widely known and
esteemed on the Continent not only as a writer but as a partisan of

progressive social movements and an enemy of authoritarian government. Despite all this, or perhaps because of it, he did not fit any better in American society than he had in his native Germany, from which he was chased in February 1933 (one newspaper called him "national vermin"), three weeks after Hitler became chancellor. He may be known today to moviegoers as the author of the novel *Professor Unrat* (i.e., "excrement"), on which the movie *The Blue Angel* is based. "My head and Marlene Dietrich's legs," as he wryly remarked.

The title of Heinrich Mann's masterpiece, *Der Untertan*, means, literally, "the underling, the one below": it connotes a slave-like person, or someone who slavers over his masters. When I first read *Man of Straw*, as it is lamely titled in English, I didn't know when it had been written. I found it searing and frightening, like acid burning through metal—yet it has a comic streak, too. I had never read anything quite like it. It made Swift look mild; you would have to go back to Juvenal for anything approaching so thorough an indictment of a society and the people who sustain it. And yet Mann seemed much saner and more authentic than Juvenal ever had. How satisfying, I thought, that someone besides Charlie Chaplin had finally "done" Hitler and the Third Reich, albeit in the guise of looking back at the previous century.

Then I learned that *Man of Straw* was begun in 1906. A few chapters had appeared in periodicals in 1914, but all publication plans were dropped at the outbreak of war. The German people, editors told Mann, could not tolerate less than reverence for the kaiser at such a critical moment. Nor, obviously, could the kaiser himself. In the autumn of 1918 the war was lost and the kaiser forced to abdicate. The Republic of Germany signed the Armistice on November 11; *Man of Straw* was published and had sold seventy-five thousand copies by December.

So the book I had admired as brilliant satire was prophecy. *Man of Straw* takes place in the 1890s, early in the reign of Wilhelm II, who was noted for militarism and authoritarian rule. To any post–World War II reader, though, the book re-creates the social and psychological conditions for the flourishing of Nazism. It is, with the regrettable benefit of history, a work that loops through eras, showing simultaneously what happened once and, like a shadow story, what happened even more disastrously again. How many more times? it inevitably asks.

Unlike his brother, Heinrich Mann was very much a political man. The two men spent years estranged over political differences, with Thomas the more conservative and patriotic, until the 1930s, when that position became untenable. *Man of Straw*'s political intrigue—shocking, dirty and ludicrous—is one of its most salient features: in a series of maneuvers of Byzantine complexity, far right and far left join forces to crush the middle. Nonetheless, Heinrich Mann knew what many other political men don't: that tyrants, like the rest of us, are trained in the nursery. Diederich Hessling, the hollow yet highly dangerous underling, becomes a caricature—the man you love to hate—as this eerie balloon of a book soars to its finish, but the psychological portrait of him at the start is deadly realism.

Diederich is a sadomasochistic toddler, terrified of his father yet proud to be abused by him because as victim he partakes of power. When his father's workmen mock him, he thinks, "I have got a beating, but from my papa. You would be glad to be beaten by him, but you are not good enough for that." He both loves and hates the insipid sentimentality of his mother and will feel confused and ambivalent about women for the rest of his life. Apart from this, there is no confusion. Diederich takes pleasure in confessing his sins and cringing. In school, he is delighted to be part of an "inhumanly indifferent" organization. "He was proud of . . . this grim power, which he felt, if only through suffering. On the headmaster's birthday flowers were placed on his desk and the blackboard. Diederich actually decorated the cane."

The novel traces Diederich's rise to power as a paper manufacturer and citizen activist in the small city of Netzig, a success won through political chicanery and slander, and inseparable from his adoration of the flamboyant emperor. The centers of narrative energy—and my own favorite passages—are the several encounters of emperor and subject, in which our loathsome hero feels a nonsensical transfer of power. With savage drollery, Mann demonstrates how this pseudo-mystical identification with power inspires allegiance to dictators. The first such meeting occurs in Berlin, where Diederich is a student and also a coward who has managed to evade military service by a bogus injury. But he belongs to the Neo-Teutons, a militaristic youth group that fosters virility and character by beer drinking. A somber demonstration by masses of the unemployed takes place along Unter der Linden:

> They reached the Castle, were driven back, and reached it again, silent and irresistible, like a river overflowing its banks . . . this turbid, dis-colored sea of poverty, rolling up in clammy waves, emitting subdued noises and throwing up, like the masts of sunken ships, poles bearing banners: "Bread! Work!" Here and there a more distinct rumbling broke out of the depths: "Bread! Work!" Swelling above the crowd it rolled off like a thunder-cloud: "Bread! Work!"

And then the emperor appears on horseback, "a young man wearing a helmet." The crowd breaks through the barriers and Diederich stumbles in front of the emperor's horse. "The Emperor gave him a piercing glance which went through him." In an effort to salute his leader, Diederich plops down in the mud. High above, the emperor laughs at him. "From the depths of his puddle Diederich stared after him, open-mouthed."

Thus begins what is, in Diederich's mind, a supernatural affinity between the two. It's not long before Diederich shapes the ends of his mustache in the twin peaks of the emperor's and learns to flash his eyes with menace at his own underlings: his mother and two sisters and the employees at the paper factory he takes over on his father's death. After the shooting of an innocent citizen by a sentry, Diederich and a group of like-minded and drunk citizens applaud military violence and dispatch a telegram to the emperor affirming that he rules by divine right. A few drinks later, and Diederich's affinity with Wilhelm has grown so potent that he forges a telegram from the emperor himself, praising the sentry and promoting him. Flashing his eyes, graced by his mustache, Diederich is so impressive that the pathetic Netzig newspaper editor says, "You look so very like—His . . ."

The next day he reads his own words in the newspaper. "Was it possible? Had he really anticipated what the Emperor would say? Was his intuition so acute? Did his brain work in unison with . . . ?" Indeed, the emperor does not deny the words. "Diederich spread out the newspaper, and gazed into its mirrored reflection of himself draped in imperial ermine."

To culminate the extraordinary union of willing slave and oblivious master, Mann concocts a whirlwind tour of the Eternal City. Diederich interrupts his honeymoon in Zurich to rush south when he hears of the emperor's diplomatic visit to Rome. In the course of trying to protect his leader and alter ego, he wards off an attack by a mad bomber: that the bomb smells of peppermint and leaves Diederich covered with tooth powder does not deflate his valor. An investigation reveals that the perpetrator, "significantly enough, was an artist."

I mention the comic aspects of *Man of Straw* because they are so deliciously satisfying, so garishly and pointedly hyperbolic. Equally hyperbolic are the caricatures of Diederich's little circle, representatives of every walk of life: the hypocritical preacher whose wayward daughter becomes Netzig's leading demimondaine, the power-hungry public prosecutor, the fanatical high-school teacher, the weak-minded newspaper editor, the stalwartly stupid old soldiers, proto-Nazis all.

But comedy is by no means the informing spirit of *Man of Straw*. Mann subtitled the novel *A history of the public soul under Wilhelm II*. In a letter to a friend, he described himself as "oppressed by this slave-like man without ideals" and wanted his book to illustrate "the slide towards 'national inhumanity,'" as indeed it does. This goal could hardly be accomplished without a foil for the slave-like Diederich, a victim of national inhumanity. The foil is the Buck family, headed by Netzig's leading citizen, old Herr Buck, a public-spirited hero of the democratic uprising of 1848, a man ready to give his life for his principles. At the novel's opening, he walks the streets magisterially, esteemed by all, a representative of the highest social ideals.

Diederich begins his systematic destruction of Buck and what he stands for by dragging Buck's son-in-law, Lauer, to court on a charge of libel. The nature of the libel is chilling, retroactively. Goaded by Diederich in a bar, Lauer suggests half-jokingly that the emperor may be tainted by Jewish blood. This is too blasphemous to be borne.

In a splendid courtroom scene, Lauer is defended by old Buck's son, Wolfgang, who is Diederich's former schoolmate and opposite number. It would be easy and neat to make Wolfgang an upstanding liberal like his father. Too easy. Instead, Mann does something exceptional with the character: Wolfgang Buck is a skeptic, a pleasure-loving freethinker, a practitioner of what today might be called situational ethics. The contrast, then, is not the familiar one of tyrant versus liberal, but the more encompassing and philosophical one of fanatic versus independent spirit.

By the end of the novel, as a result of Diederich's machinations, old Buck is ravaged in body and spirit, humiliated and ignored. There is nothing comic about it. This, Mann shows us, is what tyranny, pettiness, and demagoguery can do to intelligence, generosity, and justice. Just as Diederich's rise in the reflected glory of his emperor is charted with fine, classic inevitability, so are Buck's downfall and disgrace charted. Together their intersecting paths show a schizophrenic Germany, enlightened but bedeviled.

Alas, there is little hope to be had from the next generation. Wolfgang Buck is a lost soul in the Germany depicted, careening to self-destruction. He has neither the conviction nor the energy nor the selflessness of his father. A thoroughgoing modern spirit, he has only insight. From his mouth come the most prophetic and frightening words of all, during a discussion with Diederich about the emperor's magnetism:

> "What matters personally to each of us is not that we should really change the world very much, but that we should create in ourselves a sense of life, and a feeling that we are causing changes. That only requires talent, and the Emperor has plenty."

Diederich is horrified but Wolfgang persists: the emperor is a deliberately created and projected personality, he argues, useful for keeping people's minds off issues like bread and work. He further asks,

> "I suppose you do not know whom history will designate as the representative type of this era?"
> "The Emperor," said Diederich.
> "No," Buck replied. "The actor."

Naturally this quip has a particular tang for American readers, who have within recent memory been subjected to an actor as president. But beyond that irony vibrates the cool, canny voice of Machiavelli, drifted north. In the tradition of astute and enduring political thinkers, Mann has predicted the most insidious public development of our time, the substitution of image for character, and the pervasive falsity it generates.

Through audacity and exaggeration, this amazing novel induces terror and recognition. The pleasures it offers are not delicate but boldly startling, like expressionist painting. Since my taste usually runs to the more subtle, I have wondered why I recall it so often, with a shiver. I think it must be the author's integrity, which animates the sordid events with passion, like blessed light breaking through smog. It is the work of an artist in despair over the history of his country and its future, a man with immense powers of expression and vision, wringing the truth out of his besieged spirit to warn the world. The force of his honesty, and its cost, are irresistible.

They should be, at any rate. As we all know, the world didn't listen. Heinrich Mann lived obscurely in Hollywood, growing weaker and dependent on his brother. In 1949 he received many invitations to return to Germany (the Soviet sector), where his work was well known; he was promised honor as well as financial security. But he hesitated. And in 1950, in California, he died. Today everyone knows the work of Thomas Mann, self-styled "nonpolitical man."

Letters from
Robben Island

My brother,
   I cannot write this to my wife, who worries enough already. You must see the authorities about my health. The headaches persist, my vision is blurred, I fear something serious. I was in hospital, Cape Town, for tests, but they gave me no results and after three days sent me back to the cell. I can't lift the stones so there are beatings and spare diet punishment, which leave me weaker. Tell them my condition, ask lawyer to get treatment. Otherwise I'll die in here for sure and I must not because the children need me. Greetings to your wife and our parents. Help me, brother, my last hope, before it's too late, my words blur even as

■ ■ ■

In 2006, on a trip to South Africa, I visited Robben Island, where during the years of apartheid political prisoners were held in wretched conditions and assaulted regularly by their white guards. Robben

Island is a half hour's boat ride from Cape Town. You buy tickets at a booth, like a tourist embarking on a pleasure excursion. I felt uncomfortable visiting this once dreadful place as a tourist, but that was the only way to see it. I needn't have felt uncomfortable: the people around me were doing the same thing I was. Maybe my feeling was shame, a more private emotion. After we docked at Robben Island, which appeared flat, desolate, and sere, like a desert island of lore,

■ ■ ■

we were ushered onto buses that took us over dirt roads to the main building, a low, sand-colored structure; there we were divided into groups. Each group was assigned a guide, who was a former political prisoner.

The guide described in detail what life as a political prisoner was like: the food, the clothing, the work, the physical abuse. He said the prisoners tried to educate the white guards, who were ignorant and bigoted, and they also educated new prisoners, having resolved that their time in prison should as far as possible be useful. Regarding education, the prisoners' motto was "each one teach one." Our guide was remarkable for his lack of acrimony about his ten-year imprisonment. He said he'd

■ ■ ■

come out not enraged, as I would have expected, but convinced that only education and political action would change conditions in South Africa.

Much as I was stunned and horrified by what I saw and heard, what pierced me most deeply was the restriction on the prisoners' letters, perhaps because I am accustomed to measuring and scrutinizing my written words. The letters prisoners wrote were limited to 120 words, including the salutation and conclusion. Any extra words were cut by the censors, literally with a scissors. Often they cut material that was innocuous, either out of spite or an excess of suspicion or zeal. One hundred twenty words are not very much, especially if you're permitted to write only one

■ ■ ■

What words would someone choose to send a loved one, with only 120 at his disposal? Surely the letters, cut up as they were, must have appeared disjointed and fragmentary to those who received them. I began imagining letters the prisoners might write, 120-word letters.

For economy's sake, they might omit parts of speech, using only essentials, for instance:

> quarry move rocks blistering sun no hat
> guards beatings thirst hunger
> lights all night no reading
> piss bucket rain solitary chains sick

The problem with my imagined letters, though, was that they could never have been sent. Letters couldn't mention political activities or prison conditions, which obviously omits what was crucial to the writers. My letters would be scissored to bits.

■ ■ ■

Dear Robert,

I have sad news for you. Two nights ago, assault on prisoners because of hunger strike, not that reason is required. Customary beatings. When they were over, your father lay unconscious. Had been weak ever since he returned from three months in isolation, then injured his back, fell in quarry. Was carried to doctor but we have had no word, I fear the worst. Contact lawyers for more information, they tell us nothing. This will be hard to bear but better truth from me than official letter of lies,

who knows when. Tell your mother gently, do what you can for her.
We all grieve with you, he was brave till end, take courage until this
nightmare is

■ ■ ■

I read some books to learn more about conditions on Robben Island.
It was first used as a prison by the Portuguese in 1525; it remained a
prison later under the Dutch and British, and served as a leper colony
and an insane asylum.

Years before apartheid was dismantled, I heard the African American novelist John Williams speak about the brutal South African
regime to a mostly white audience. His bitter closing words: Who
here knows how to spell Robben Island?

Now that Nelson Mandela's presidency has come and gone, as has
the Truth and Reconciliation Commission, people are probably even
less aware of Robben Island. It still interests me, though. Besides the
conditions, it's the restrictions on the letters.

■ ■ ■

Or they might expand a bit more:
Dearest, you ask what life is like: quarry hammer stone to gravel
  rain wind no hat no shoes socks no stopping singing talking
  Today shovel trip fall limp doctor back to work aches back legs
  mealy-meal sandy, flies in bowl night warders beating strip search-
ing shouting no newspapers radio try studying waiting for books censors
  eyes sting need spectacles lights burn all night sleep damp mat concrete
floor Enough. Write me of you, children. Colin in school still? little one
read yet? Your parents sisters brother? Roof fixed? You my love? Your
knee? In my dreams always
  16 words to spare love wait for me patience end will come faith
  forever your Joshua

. . .

words aren't much, especially if you're permitted only one letter every six months: this during the worst period, 1962–1966, described in Neville Alexander's *Robben Island Dossier*, a 1984 report to the international community, as the "years of hell." From 1967 to 1970, the rules relaxed marginally; one letter a month. (In 1971–1972 treatment grew harsher again, in what the report calls a "pendulum policy.") What words, given such limitations? Poets have thrived on formal limits, meter and rhyme and the rigorous rules of sonnets, sestinas and such. Freedom within certain boundaries is the principle behind those forms (as behind some forms of government), and great poems have resulted. However, I doubt that the Robben Island

. . .

prisoners would have found any virtues in the rules imposed on them.

Indeed, I can't imagine what they might have written, besides inquiring after the health and welfare of their families, which would make for rather dull letters. *Dearest Mother, I'm doing well, my foot is all healed. How are you and my sisters? Has Nellie's asthma improved? Did you manage to get the TV working again?* I couldn't compose such letters. Could the prisoners? They must have composed in their heads other letters, the ones they wished they could write. Those were the letters I was imagining. But as I did, I developed doubts about whether I could even imagine them. What did I know about prison life, never

. . .

My dear Mother,
Don't worry about me, I'm doing fine. My foot is all healed from the pick-axe and I'm getting strong muscles. I think of you each day and pray

for your health and that of my father. The men here help me as I am the youngest. Please ask the lawyer about my enrollment in university. If you can find the money and he obtains permission I can continue my studies here and complete my degree. We have classes when we can, after the day's work, history and economics, but books are scarce and censored. I miss your good cooking—today I found a horsefly in the soup! Luckily he did not drink much.

    Your loving son,
    William

▪ ▪ ▪

The buses took us to the quarries where the prisoners worked, huge, sandy open spaces where they crushed stones and sometimes moved piles of stones uselessly from one place to another, as was the practice in Nazi concentration camps. Other work, I learned from my reading, included chopping wood, repairing roads and dragging seaweed from the beaches. We saw the small bungalows where the white warders lived. This part of the island, far from the prisoners' quarters, was not desertlike, but rather resembled a barracks village with uniform houses in uniform rows, each with a bit of yard outside, even a few swing sets, a wagon, a bicycle; the guards lived there with their families, so the yards must have

▪ ▪ ▪

been used by children. There were also sports fields for the guards. Nevertheless, it didn't resemble a place where anyone would want to live or raise a family.

    The guide led us through the barracks or dormitories where the political prisoners slept; we saw the tiny concrete cells containing only the buckets used as toilets. We saw Nelson Mandela's cell. I was expecting that this would induce awe, as if an aura of Mandela's courage and resilience still inhabited the room. But I had to admit, to my chagrin, that the cell was merely an empty, bleak space like the others.

We saw the large mess hall—long wooden tables and benches, and on the walls, charts of the precise

• • •

What did I know about prison life, never mind a South African prison? True, I had read books and talked to many South Africans, including several who'd left the country in frustration and disgust. A writer should be able to imagine herself into any situation—that's what imagination is for. Even so, I felt a sense of presumption. Did I have the right to attempt these letters? Would they sound absurdly ignorant?

Such doubts assail all writers no matter what they're writing. But they felt particularly powerful to me, maybe because South Africa was so far away and the prisoners' lives and struggles so remote from my own experience. And then I was suspicious of my reasons for visiting Robben

• • •

My son,

I know it's a heavy burden to be without your father, and your mother not well. Remember how proud I am that you're behaving like a man, though I wish you might have enjoyed your boyhood longer. Here you are with me constantly. Thoughts of you, your mother and sisters keep me strong, counting the days until I see you again—978. Meanwhile take care of your mother and sisters and above all, keep at your studies. When you are tempted to fall into idleness or despair, struggle against it with all your might. Never be ashamed that your father is in prison—you understand the cause. See that your mother gets some rest and don't let her

• • •

wall charts of the precise amounts of food allotted for each meal: a few ounces of bread, soup made of powder and water, mealy-meal (maize) and tea. The charts listed quantities of food for each racial group, with Africans receiving the smallest amount. Five diets were cited in the *Robben Island Dossier*: A for European females, B for European males, C for nonwhite females, D for Indian and Colored (mixed-race) males, and F—an all-maize diet—for black African males. Indians and Colored people got extra sugar for coffee. The "spare diet" punishment was boiled maize and soup powder in water twice daily; "three meals" punishment meant no food at all that day. Frequently the "meals" included sand and insects.

■ ■ ■

suspicious of my reasons for visiting Robben Island and of my reactions on seeing the rock quarries, the mess hall, Mandela's cell and all the rest. Was there some secret prurient thrill in being so close to suffering, a suffering I hadn't had to endure but wanted a visceral inkling of by proxy, by way of others' suffering? I've never wanted to visit Auschwitz or Dachau or the other German camps now transformed into tourist attractions. I even consider the transformation of these places into tourist attractions a form of vulgarity. On the other hand, people are naturally curious and have a right to see the residue of history, which might serve some educational purpose. Do those tourists who visit

■ ■ ■

As with food, clothing was allotted by race. Until 1970 only Colored people and Indians were issued long pants, shoes, socks, a shirt and jacket for the work in the quarries. In the early "years of hell," and indeed until 1970, black African prisoners had no shoes, socks, long pants or warm clothes to protect them against the winter winds coming off the sea. They wore shorts all year round. Colored people and

Indians had hats, Africans a cap. No one had hats suitable for rain or the sizzling summer sun. They were given only a few blankets in cold weather, described in the report as "old, thin, dirty, smelly." In 1974 prisoners were issued underwear for the first time.

■ ■ ■

Dearest Mother,

Madiba was put in solitary today, on my account. I stopped work, my head pounding so badly in the hot sun, the guard came to strike me, as expected. I only needed a moment's rest. But I didn't expect that Madiba, working alongside me in the quarry, would step in. He grasped the guard's raised arm and said calmly to let me alone, I was just a boy and doing the best I could. Then three guards attacked us both and dragged him off. I feel very bad about this. Everything feels different without him, morale lower. He kept us going. I hope he's back soon. If you can get word out maybe they'll release him—his reputation.

■ ■ ■

tourists who visit Auschwitz or other camps become more humane as a result? Who can say? In any case, I could visualize the barracks, the smokestacks, the piles of shoes well enough. I had read plenty about them, and reading, for me, makes things as vivid as actual seeing, or more so. I'd never wanted to write from the point of view of those prisoners. Maybe the South African prisoners' experiences drew me because although they were more remote geographically, they happened during my lifetime. While I was attending school, sleeping in a bed, dreaming of future opportunities, others were breaking rocks, getting beaten, and sleeping in narrow concrete cells. Was I seeking some sort of atonement for my privileges?

■ ■ ■

Many of the island's political prisoners tried to pursue their studies and to keep up with events on the outside, but this was overwhelmingly difficult. No newspapers or radio were allowed, and study privileges were withdrawn as a punishment for any perceived misbehavior. Prisoners could not apply to university programs unless they had enough money in a bank account; the installment plan available to ordinary students was not offered. Because it was hard to study right after the day's work, prisoners asked to be allowed to sleep for a few hours after work, then resume their studies at night, but no reading was permitted after eleven o'clock, even though the lights were kept on all night. Prisoners had to reapply

∙ ∙ ∙

for study privileges each year. No law studies were permitted; no scientific journals were available. The number of books was restricted, and reference works and encyclopedias were unavailable. Often prisoners waited months for books they had ordered; they weren't permitted to lend books among themselves. But by far the worst restriction was censorship: no material including references to Marxism, Lenin, Russia, China, Cuba, socialism, communism, revolution, civil war, violence, Africa, anti-apartheid literature or political literature written by blacks. Nonetheless, despite these limitations, prisoners held their own classes.

There was more, much more, in the *Robben Island Dossier* about the atrocious prison conditions, but what I keep coming back to when I try to imagine life there are the 120 words.

∙ ∙ ∙

When I was a kid riding the New York City subways, there was an ad we all laughed at, advertising a stenography school. U cn ri 120 wpm & gt a gd jb ... Stenography is long gone. Now we have 144-character Twitter messages, emoticons and abbreviations like omg, btw, lol, which, compared with the 120-word limit on prisoners' correspondence, seem a cartoonish parody of those proscriptions.

People can return to their studies once released, and if they're fortunate like our guide, their bodies can heal from the wounds inflicted; they can eat better foods. With effort they may even overcome acrimony. But the things they might have written in the letters will never be said, or sent.

■ ■ ■

My darling,

Do you remember the summer day soon after we met, we walked down the road out of town, then sat in the grass and talked, you told me about yourself and I told you, we lay down in the grass, you said, Wait, I can't do this unless it will be truly important. I thought, I can persuade her, I know how with pretty words, then I looked at your face, something there touched me deeply, I said, Yes, it will be very important, and so it still is my darling. You didn't know then I was political but can you wait? I fall asleep thinking of how you looked, your body against the grass that day, your

■ ■ ■

At some point I realized that all my imagined letters were written by noble, patient prisoners, prisoners who kept faith in their political convictions, who were confident that they would one day be released to carry on the struggle, or if not, that others would carry it on for them. How naïve. Surely some prisoners weren't so confident or high-minded; surely many must have despaired and nourished hatred and been broken in spirit. After all, that was what the prison sentences and the prison conditions were designed to accomplish. We remember only the heroes, but it is ingenuous to expect everyone to be heroic, even with the study groups and the singing and the example of heroic companions around them.

● ● ●

This will be my last letter. Think of me as dead. Even if I get out of here alive, even if you see me walking around, I'll be dead. My body, nearly destroyed, somehow keeps on, a husk that works, eats, shits, and sleeps. As for the rest, what I used to call the spirit, it no longer exists. Let the others keep fighting, if they can. I hope only that the next beating will bring the end. I haven't even used up all my words, but there is nothing left to say.

● ● ●

Dear Steven,

I thought at the beginning that I would use whatever time I could to continue my studies, but that ambition is gone. It takes too long to wait for books, and in the white authorities' infinite wisdom they don't allow us to borrow books. Can you believe that? Of course you can. We can believe anything of them. So I've learned nothing here in prison except to hate more and better than before. It takes all my strength to keep from striking the guards with the pickax, I've gotten so brutal. When I tried that, months ago, they put me in solitary with no food and slimy water, so I haven't tried again. Not that I hope to

● ● ●

Next month: *stay alive. I just don't want to die raving mad. The company of the others keeps me sane. The strong ones encourage me, the leaders are superhuman in their will to survive, but for me it's no use. Some of them even sing at night, though that's not permitted and they're usually punished for it. I like hearing the singing. Maybe death will come some night to the sounds of their voices. That would be better than dying to the sounds of the guards' vile white voices shouting, or the sound of blows on flesh, our most common music.*

Of course nothing like this would ever have gotten past the prison censors, not one word, far less 120.

■ ■ ■

In 2006, years after I heard John Williams's bitter words, I heard quite
different ones from a South African woman I danced with at a gala
celebration at a community center in Langa, a township near Cape
Town. I was visiting my husband, who was leading a group of college
students traveling and studying in various countries. A party was held
at the end of their stay in Langa, with delicious food contributed by
local people, live music and dancing, everyone exhilarated. I didn't
know the woman—we just grabbed each other in the general frolick-
ing and spun wildly around the room. "If we were doing this twelve
years ago," she said, panting for breath, "we'd be put in jail."

The Piano

I still have the Baldwin baby grand piano my parents gave me as a high school graduation present decades ago. All through my adult life, every time I moved I took it with me—no easy feat with a piano so large—or else found it a suitable temporary lodging. The piano has accompanied me from Brooklyn to Philadelphia to Boston and is now settled in Manhattan, where it occupies a good part of the living room. Once, I went to Italy for a year, and for that year I asked my sister to shelter it. When I returned I found a few paper clips lodged inside among the strings and I heatedly accused my sister of not taking proper care of the piano, which in retrospect seems an odd over-reaction on my part: just a few clips, after all.

It's not clear to me why I've held on to the piano for so long and continue to play it, considering that I no longer play well or, to be candid, with much enthusiasm. It's not that I love it so much. I hardly love it at all, at this point. (This has nothing to do with loving music. I listen to music as much as ever and am enchanted by fine pianists. It's only my own playing that has ceased to enchant me.)

The piano is a handsome piece of furniture, a warm cherry wood, still fairly sleek and shiny—it would be even shinier if I polished it—and impressive, especially when the lid is opened to its full extension. But beauty alone can't account for my inability to let it go. I find it hard, in general, to stop doing anything enjoyable once I've started, which is one reason I've never tried hard drugs: I know what would happen. Habit, as Proust noted, is the most constricting of traps. Playing the piano is a benign, not dangerous or illegal habit, but even so, in my case it has gone on far too long; the habit has outlived the enjoyment it once yielded. Luckily my living room is large enough to accommodate the old piano, yet every so often I gaze at it in all its grandeur and imagine to what better uses I might put that space.

I was the musical child of a musical mother. She sang and played the piano (better by ear than from a score), the accordion, the banjo, and the mandolin. I played by ear when I was quite young, which prompted my parents to give me piano lessons starting at the age of six. I studied with various teachers until I left home to go to college, and by then I played pretty well, though not spectacularly well. My first teacher was called Miss Milady, and I thought of her as Miss Melody, which suited her: she was a lady of lilts and frills and trills, pink cheeks and gray curls adorned with a pink ribbon. My mother took me to her apartment, where she served shortbread cookies. Subsequent teachers came to my house and were more serious and professional—a hulking Eastern European with wild hair, whom I always pictured in a flowing velvet cape and, finally, a high school teacher who was a superb pianist and with whom I was a little bit in love. He suggested that I work towards a musical career. But I never wanted to be a pianist. I just liked playing and playing well, and I particularly liked having this teacher's full attention and approval for an hour or more every week.

I don't know what musical aspirations my parents had for me; they never articulated any, but rather encouraged me to be a schoolteacher, which also held no attraction. In any case, they bought me the piano at great cost, over a thousand dollars, a lot of money at that time, certainly a lot for them to spend all at once. I can't remember whether it was their idea or if I asked for it; nor do I recall the doubtless humbler instrument I played before the Baldwin joined our household. That is, I remember vaguely what it looked like (black, unobtrusive) but not how it felt and sounded, which is what matters in a piano. I remember only that the new piano, bought under the guidance of that final, so charming, teacher, arrived with fanfare and I was thrilled to possess such a large and imposing object. At sixteen one does not own very much, and certainly nothing on the scale of a baby grand piano.

Maybe it was this, the pride of ownership of so splendid and expensive an instrument, that made me start lugging it around when I embarked on my adult life. Without regular lessons, I tried to maintain some sort of practice schedule; I would play over and over the pieces I'd been working on when my lessons stopped. But that spurt of ambition didn't last. I was caught up in other pursuits and played less and less. Every few years I'd have an access of rigor and a spate of practicing. But it was boring to keep playing the same old pieces again and again. I tried learning new ones, but since even in my best years I was a poor sight reader, this was a struggle. After fumbling through some new Mozart sonata or Bach fugue, I would revert to show tunes or folk music, which I could play tolerably well. Meanwhile my performances of those old classical pieces—eroding daily under my fingers—were painful to listen to, a sorry reminder of the gap between my past and present ability.

So young, and already there was loss. It's crushing to lose the capacity to do something we once did well, but we usually don't have to endure such losses until middle age: think of baseball players, ballet dancers, mountain climbers. Still, those losses come with the territory; they're inevitable and expected. My loss was entirely preventable, if only I had practiced. But I didn't want to practice. I wanted to play sporadically and yet play well. This, as any pianist can tell you, is not possible.

In one of my more rigorous moods, I undertook to learn ragtime.

Scott Joplin. His pieces, I found, I could learn pretty easily and I could listen to my efforts without cringing, even with some pleasure. I felt an immediate and instinctive affinity with Joplin's music. It reminded me of playing Bach, except that Joplin was predictable while Bach was not. After learning several of Joplin's pieces, I could tell right away where he was headed in each, what chords and harmonic patterns would turn up. This was comforting, reassuring. Bach was totally unpredictable—I never could tell what moves he would make next, and I found this unsettling, not to mention difficult. Of course that very unpredictability is part and parcel of his genius, but to a pianist like me, it was exasperating.

So I've made my way through almost all of the works of Scott Joplin, and now, when I'm frustrated by my ever-dwindling ability to play a Bach fugue, I play ragtime. I could say I've become a specialist, like doctors and lawyers. But even with the Joplin pieces, I notice that my fingers have forgotten the intervals they once found so readily. I can get the shadings right, the feel of the music, but I get tangled in a flurry of wrong notes, the most rudimentary kind of error, like a doctor who can perform surgery but can't locate a vein for a simple injection. Those wrong notes are unbearable, because I know exactly how the music should sound. I hear it in my head, and in my head my fingers can make it sound perfect.

The wrong notes are even more galling because I harbor a secret faith that one day, miraculously, I'll get my old proficiency back: my fingers will be as nimble as they are in my silent mental performances. They'll be the fingers of my teenaged self, flitting confidently over the keys, making beautiful, evocative music. I'm constantly surprised and disappointed that this doesn't happen. Playing the piano is not, alas, like riding a bicycle.

So long as I keep the piano, for whatever muddled reasons, I feel obliged to keep it tuned and in good condition. Out of respect for the piano itself and for my parents, both long dead, who left it trustingly in my care. Maintaining it is part of the enigmatic bargain I've evidently struck with them, a pact to honor their belief in my imputed talent. All those lessons, all that faith, not to mention money, invested in my piano playing. Obviously my parents no longer care. Even if I believed in an afterlife in which my parents keep an eye out from above, given the vicissitudes of my life, the piano would be low priority on their list of concerns about me. And yet I remain in thrall to it, most likely forever.

The piano is old now and, like aging people, needs regular professional attention, which I provide, within reason, as my piano tuner advises. Every few months he sends me a printed card saying it's time to have the piano tuned. I call him and he comes. I enjoy his visits; he's full of conversation. Also blind, as a number of piano tuners are, though he navigates through his busy life very efficiently; he lost his sight in his early twenties and so knows what the world looks like. He says the piano is in excellent shape for its years, still lively and exuberant, no signs of dementia except for one intermittently stuck key, which I must attend to. It would fetch a good price, the piano tuner says, several times more than the original purchase price. Not that he advises me to sell it. No, he suggests expensive and complicated procedures that would make it last even longer, maybe even outlast me as it outlasted my parents, the original donors.

Following his advice, I recently had the piano cleaned, inside and out, and now he says I should have it regulated, so as to—and here I paraphrase—prevent the action from getting sluggish, keep the keys responding properly, and keep the parts relating as they were originally designed to do. Also, the hammers would benefit by being filed. I don't have a clear sense of what all this means, but I suppose I'll do it one of these days. Such upkeep costs more than the piano did.

After the piano tuner's visits, I vow to practice more, now that the piano has been revitalized, but after a couple of weeks I slip back into my old habits, playing just a few hours on weekends, which feels like a form of blasphemy. In my best piano playing years I practiced at least an hour and a half a day. I suspect that I would play better and more often if I had an appreciative audience. I'm unduly dependent on encouragement in whatever I do. Obviously an audience is out of the question, so now and then, to spur myself on, I make believe I'm playing for enthusiastic listeners, and this does improve my playing slightly. My parents were my best audience, so I often try to imagine them listening. They wouldn't be hard to impress; they might not detect the wrong notes or be appalled by them—anyway, Joplin is easy to fake. See, I tell them, I'm still playing the piano you bought me.

They gave it to me as an act of faith; they expected me to play it, and I do. I'm like the girl with the red shoes, who couldn't stop dancing until they cut her feet off. Except that she had talent, and whatever talent I once had has evaporated. No, on second thought, I suppose talent itself doesn't disappear; what disappears is its outward expression, without which talent lies dormant. I wouldn't go so far as to have my hands chopped off simply so I could stop playing the piano, but sometimes I do wish I could sell it, or just give it away.

But I can't. Someday I might have the urge to sit down and play a Joplin rag, and I won't be able to do that unless I keep practicing every few days. And there's always the chance that my fingers might be suddenly transformed into the fleet fingers of my youth. It's only through an evil spell cast by time that I can't make the music sound the way I hear it in my mind, the way my fingers play it in my mind.

Altogether I have too much to lose: the tangible, audible link to those early gratifying hours at the piano, feeling the happy sense of proficiency; the link to the myth of miraculous recovery of what is lost; and the link to my parents, who gave the piano its first home and listened to me play it. So there it sits in the living room, grand and magisterial. Mine. It was given to me to play, and so I do. Chances are I will play it until my dying day, unless my hands grow stiff and palsied. That would be a legitimate excuse to stop; in that event, my parents, wherever they are, could hardly expect me to continue.

Street Food

Why, I've often wondered, is New York's symbol a wholesome red apple, when the more obvious choice would be the blue and yellow umbrella of a Sabrett's hot dog stand, an irresistible beacon shimmering in the wind?

That New York is the great American walking city is well known. It's also the great American ruminating city: we think on our feet—chewing all the way. In Manhattan you're never far from food, and for me, nothing about city life has quite the racy, almost defiant allure of eating on the street. With a hot dog in hand I become jaunty and carefree, young and blithe-spirited.

As a child in Brooklyn I dreamed of emigrating to Manhattan and imagined I'd have to acquire a suave urbanity in order to succeed there, or even to survive. I was not entirely wrong. But I was wrong in thinking urbanity was entirely suave. In fact urbanity, New York style, has its rough spots and leaves plenty of room for earthy indulgence

Eating on the street makes that statement as plainly as any T-shirt: it announces that I rate pleasure higher than dignity, that the cares and proprieties of adulthood haven't beaten me down. Away with sedate lunches—napkins and silverware and waiters reciting the daily specials. I'm still a child of the streets.

Let me be very clear: this has nothing to do with the charms of al fresco dining, or gracious picnics in Central Park, or even the ubiquitous muffins (cake in disguise) and other sanctimonious snacks you can pick up in salad bars and carry out. I mean the real stuff: zesty food that's prepared ("cooked" might be an overstatement) and served—I use the word loosely—from big aluminum carts by vendors, nowadays many of them Middle Eastern, bringing a touch of the exotic and sautéing their savory, aromatic dishes with deft, swift movements. They've wheeled their carts through perilous traffic to their assigned corners and can sometimes be seen trudging home with them at twilight or attaching them to the backs of small cars, having nourished our reveries yet another day. For street food is the comforting companion to a solitary walk: it's right there when you want it, and unlike a human companion, it enlivens your daydreams and never interrupts.

My déclassé tastes may be partly nostalgia for the days when food vendors would traipse over the sands of Brighton Beach with trays slung from their shoulders by wide canvas bands and resting on their stomachs, like cigarette girls in nightclubs, also a long-gone amenity. They'd stop right by your blanket: rarely has hunger been so readily appeased. Or when George the Good Humor man's white truck turned the corner every afternoon at four thirty, scattering our punchball game and supplying pops or Dixie ice-cream cups to get us through the hour and a half until dinner. (The Good Humor truck permanently parked alongside the Guggenheim Museum can still instantly evoke my childhood, madeleine style.)

Nostalgia is far from the whole story, though. People gather in cities in the frank and urgent desire for company. And where people gather, food must follow. Every major city has its distinctive street food: in Amsterdam it's raw herrings, in Paris *pommes frites*. In Mexico

City, women sit at braziers beside heaped-up tortillas like stacks of giant coins, frying them one by one and wrapping up savory fillings. But only in New York, fittingly, has street food reached such a pitch of multicultural diversity.

If Henry James was aghast, over a century ago, at the pageant of raucous immigrants swarming his once-genteel New York streets, hawking their grubby wares in thick syllables, how much more horrified would he be at the motley bands surrounding the bright umbrellas that fringe office buildings and hospitals and universities, waiting to ease their souls with gyros or souvlaki, cheeseburgers, Afghan chicken, knishes, Philly steaks or Italian sausages, eggplant sandwiches, crushed ice oozed with a rainbow of Latino syrups, over-sized bagels and doughnuts, or pretzels pimpled with salt and slathered with mustard?

Sixth Avenue is street food heaven. Heading east from Columbus Circle, then down Sixth to Bryant Park, the ruminating walker can make a meal from soup to nuts: six varieties of soup (all natural, no preservatives) and roasted nuts whose honeyed, swoony odor wafts over a half-block radius. The fruit stands displaying everything from grapes to pomegranates for dessert are almost too virtuous to be included in any tribute to disreputable food. But virtue has its niche, even on the street.

A curious enterprise, Potato King, raises a philosophical question. Proclaiming "Potato Is Healthy," it adorns that humble base with chili, spinach and cheese, sour cream and, for the incorrigibly pious, yogurt or cottage cheese. The potatoes look delicious but, alas, unwieldy. I would argue that they go too far for genuine street food. As do the stands that offer whole meals: chicken and beef with rice, lamb kofta, even salad. Not to mention the soup.

Cooking up stews and soups on the sidewalks of New York is clever and audacious, I must admit. And yet the appeal of street food is that it fits nonchalantly in the hand—no Styrofoam required. Its particular genius rests in design as well as tang: witness a moderately complex dish like shish kebab or falafel made suitable for strolling. But lamb kofta, salad on the side, demands that you sit on a stone ledge and use a fork, and while that has its pleasures, especially on warm days, it's a far cry from a New York walk punctuated by munches. No, street food must be eaten with a devil-may-care airiness or in an absent-minded daze. It must give instant gratification with no effort whatsoever. Soup asks too much concentration.

For all its unassuming earthiness, though, street food keeps some mysteries. Where do the carts go overnight? Who fills them each morning? How does the unending supply of rolls and sausages and whatnot fit in those small spaces? What goes into that powerful brew from which the hot dogs are speared? And exactly how long have they been floating in it? Who knows? Who cares? *Bon appétit.*

Absence Makes the Heart

A close friend moves away. Someone important. Say your life is a soup, then she is a vital ingredient. The soup will still be nourishing, appetizing, but different. Something's missing, you'd say if you tasted it. She too feels the loss. How will she manage without your conversations? she says. Still, she goes, for reasons of necessity. Quite far, to the other end of the earth. And she doesn't write. Nothing but a card, that is, giving her address.

You think of what it was like having her around. Around the corner, actually, so that often you'd run into her on the street, going to her car, maybe. A huge mustardy-green sedan, one of those ancient boatlike cars. She was very particular about having passengers fasten their seat belts even in the back seat, which was out of character—she wasn't especially cautious or finicky. Or only in certain ways. She maneuvered the car through the city with deft grace, with moderate aggression. She was good with machines, though she seemed, deceptively, the sort of gentle, elegant, sometimes ethereal person who wouldn't be. She was one of the first people you knew to use a computer and used it with delight, long, long ago, when it was a novelty; when you asked her what something typed on a computer would look like, she sent you a very brief letter that read, This is what it looks like, then signed her name. That was in character.

You would sit in her fifth-floor apartment with the French doors open, the breeze blowing in. The living room was cool and airy and colorful. You sat on one of several secondhand couches with print throws in muted colors, amber, lemon, mustardy colors. The room was filled, though not cluttered, with odd and distinctive objects you find now, regrettably, you cannot recall one by one, as well as with piles of books and papers. On the verge of messiness, but not quite. Neatly messy. And paintings she had painted herself, in chalky tones, of flat, disingenuous figures in rooms with mirrors and double images.

On a table in front of the couch she would set out neatly arranged snacks, wedges of cheese, crackers, small clusters of grapes. She would snip clusters of grapes off the bunch with a scissors—this you watched, sitting on a stool in her narrow kitchen while she prepared the snacks, poured the wine or made the tea. She was fussy about tea the way she was fussy about seat belts: the water had to be boiled. Very hot was not good enough, she said. It tasted right only if the water came to a boil. In restaurants, she said, she would ask specifically that the water be boiled, but could always tell when her request had not been honored.

Back in the living room her gentle voice murmured sly, hilarious, bitter words. Your topics of conversation were men, children, work, books, clothing, food, travel, parents, money, politics, mutual friends, pretty much in that order. She spoke so softly that it took a moment to grasp how outrageous and rebellious her words were. There was this unexpectedness in her, the subversive words belying a compliant surface. Also, unexpectedly, she was often late. Not insultingly, just mildly late, but always unexpectedly because her precision and considerateness suggested the habit of promptness.

You miss all of this. You wait for a letter about her new life—this is before the days when email replaced letters. Finally you write; after a while she answers. You don't know her handwriting well—there has been no need for letters before—and studying this new representation of her, you feel puzzled. The handwriting is clear and fairly conventional, quite out of character. You write back, she doesn't answer. You are beginning to revise your naïve notions of in character, out of character.

A year later she sends a card announcing that she'll be back for a few months. She resumes your close friendship as if there had been no absence, and no absence of letters. You bring up the subject of her not writing. She explains that things have been difficult. In some ways. While in other ways, things have gone very well. She is so far away, she says, so stunned by the move and the distance, that in order to keep her equilibrium in the far place she cannot allow herself to think of anything or anyone from the old place. If she did, she would feel her feet were rooted on different continents and she might very well topple over or split down the middle. Therefore she cannot stay in touch. But on her intermittent returns, you can resume your close friendship just as before.

This is odd and puzzling. But, very well.

A year passes and again she returns for a while. Another year, another return, the close friendship once more resuming as if there had been no absence. You try to "catch up." But many things happen in a year, many changes. Every few months your own outlook on life shifts, you learn some hard and required lesson that makes you a slightly different person. The soup that is your life has a different taste, different ingredients, is thicker or thinner. Presumably the same is happening to her. How to take account of these shifts, let her know who you are now? You cannot sum up each lesson like a homily; you can, if you try, recount the events that led to the lessons, but that takes time and her time is limited; there is the present to enjoy; and it is tedious to narrate a series of small events whose vividness and importance are bound to the moment they took place. The pacing is what matters. The organic accumulation that is change. Had she been present to witness the small events succeeding each other, there would be no need to present the lessons in a package—they would be self-evident.

There is of course the telephone. You can call anywhere now, easily, even the other end of the earth. But you feel she doesn't wish to hear from you. She said it pains her to think of people from her old place. The fact that she does not wish to think of you, that she chooses to forget you for long periods and is able to do so, is painful and makes you angry. Naturally, you have passed permanently out of existence for many people, as many have for you—that is not troubling. But you cannot understand the shift taking place in her mind that enables her to banish you from existence for a year at a time, then to return and feel as close as before. This process you cannot understand shakes your sense of solidity: how odd to move in and out of existence in her mind while you feel so strongly your continuous bodily existence. This process she is capable of is what places distance between you, even more so than the actual expanse of land and ocean.

You have, of course, other friends who live far away. But they always did. They were never part of the soup but rather a snack, a special treat. Moreover, with other faraway friends, you exchange letters, even phone calls. Or not, as the case may be. With other faraway friends, there is a tacit agreement on how to keep in touch. They do not put you out of their minds; they call or write now and then, saying, I was thinking of you and thought I'd call, or write. Or, Something important is happening that I must tell you. In this case, anything might be happening and she feels no need to tell you.

On the next visit, when she calls to announce that she is back, happy to hear your voice and ready to resume as if there had been no absence, you respond with anger. How can she expect, and so on and so on. She cries. She has no excuse. Things have been very hard, complicated, almost indescribably so. She repeats that she cannot think of anyone or anything here, she would be in two places at once, and so on. At her weeping, your anger dissipates. Very well, you will resume as if there had been no absence. You try to tell her some large things that have happened to you and how you are a different person because of them. But you are also the same person, the person who can tell her such things and have them understood. She listens and responds in the same gentle, sly, comprehending manner, as satisfying as before.

Still, you come away unsettled, confused about the continuity of identity, about the nature of friendship, of existence, even—the way, in her view, we can slip into and out of existence for each other. Not a congenial notion for you, though it apparently works for her.

When she leaves this time you try with, yes, a touch of vindictiveness to do as she does, not think about her, but you do not readily succeed. You wonder about her difficulties, what her house looks like, what kind of car she drives, who are the new people she thinks about daily. She has told you some and you imagine the rest; what is missing from your imaginings are things like snipped grapes, thoroughly boiled tea, and furniture. The details that do not, by their nature, get spoken of when time is short, and without which our images of people are wan.

After a while, though, you realize you are succeeding in your effort. You do think of her occasionally, but with an alien detachment. You think, but you do not care. It is as if she does not exist. She is not on the other end of the earth at all; she is nowhere, her life static, in abeyance until she returns next year to resume her existence. You do not especially look forward to her return or miss her anymore—the soup changes all the time, and that old soup of which she was a vital ingredient is a thing of the past—but when she returns, you will be happy to see her and to care anew, as deeply as always, to take up your close friendship as before, as if there had been no absence.

This is a lesson. This is how you are different now.

Meditations in Time of War

I've spent a good part of my adult life unraveling the tangled weave of my childhood. I'd like to get rid of the shreds and knotty bits, the misconceptions I grew up with, and weave a reasonable adulthood out of newer, truer strands. When the mess overwhelms me, I fret that I'm wasting precious time, Penelope-like, unweaving and reweaving. Throw it all out. But maybe it's the fated task of my adult life. Come to think of it, weaving is too delicate an image. It's a vast excavation, a dig for the shards of my early delusions. These are no treasures I'm seeking, to illuminate a past civilization. They're trash.

Not that my childhood was bad. It wasn't bad at all. Maybe even too good. The period in which I chanced to grow up, the late 1940s and 1950s in Brooklyn, New York, was a brief time warp of optimism and assumed innocence in the otherwise bloody, tattered fabric of history. It doesn't offer much of shock value; my childhood's shocks were delayed, aftershocks of recognition that keep coming, again and again, of how different the world and human beings are from what I was led to believe. Or chose to believe. Or still believe against all evidence.

The default mode back then was decency, the self-satisfied, narrow, blinkered decency of the postwar years. Bad behavior of any kind was a departure from this mode. My mother, a good-hearted peacemaker, practiced virtue and was shocked at any defection, from the Japanese bombing of Pearl Harbor to a neighbor's neglecting to invite her to a party: both perpetrators were forever cast out of her good graces. Her pained indignation was contagious and curiously satisfying. My response to adversity large and small became aggrieved surprise. That wasn't how things were supposed to be. How dare anyone flout the rules? How could they go against human nature?

Children can be notoriously cruel, and I encountered and probably doled out my fair share of cruelty. Yet even this didn't change my notion that the world was meant to be benign. Even more, it was supposed to give me what I wanted. When the world didn't comply, I was bewildered, resentful. It took some time before I realized that the odd component of this dynamic wasn't the bad behavior or the world's intransigence but my constant surprise. Even now it lingers. I can't seem to grasp that adversity is in the scheme of things, *is* the scheme of things. I don't like this bewilderment, I can even laugh at it, but it's stubbornly there.

I could catalogue a dozen forms of instilled delusion from those years. There was the imparting or withholding of information on an arbitrary, need-to-know basis, that is, I never told you, because I thought it might upset you. There was the assumption that it was indelicate to mention serious personal problems, so that nothing dire came to light until it reached crisis proportions and was beyond help, and then came a moaning and tearing of hair. But the delusion that feels most pungent, and may be the foundation of the others, has to do with the war. World War II, for those for whom "the war" might be ambiguous.

Yet the war we're presently engaged in, the war that is so much with us, the war the government with its usual verbal sloppiness likes to call the war on terror, may well come to overshadow what I call "the war." (They'd do better calling it the war on terrorism. A war on terror, existential terror, can never be won; it is part of our human state.) Of course it is that new war that's reviving memories of the old one.

I was too young to be aware of the war. Friends born a few years earlier remember following the progress of battles with colored pins on maps hung on their living room walls—although I doubt that my parents would have done that in any event. All I knew of the war was standing in the ration line holding my mother's hand as she clutched a small booklet of tickets, and saving the wires that came wound around the fluted paper lids of milk bottles. I do remember the celebration when it was over, after we dropped the bomb, though I didn't know about the bomb itself. I knew only that I was part of a great parade on a country road, for it was summertime and we were in the country, and I walked alongside my mother, who rhythmically shook a tambourine amid a crowd of other shakers in paroxysms of glee, and on the dirt road were cow pats to watch out for, about the same circumference as the tambourines though with no bells attached.

With the postwar exuberance and relief came a tacit conspiracy—if conspiracy seems too strong a word, let's say collective will—to put the war behind us, to smother it with silence, the way you hastily fling a blanket to crush a fire. To move on, as we say today. "Let it go" and "move on" are our mantras; we mustn't cling morbidly to the past; we are a nation psychically on the move, divesting ourselves of history to invest in a future that itself will be swiftly left behind, an endless caravan never pausing to gaze back over the landscape just traversed.

Looking back, I'm struck not only by the absence of talk about the war—and I was always lurking and listening for clues to the grown-up world—but by the clarity of the air, no thickness or foul mist hinting at what the war had demonstrated about human nature or human capacities, specifically the capacity for brutality. The capacity for heroism was public and evident: the air was sweet with triumphalism, the triumph of decency over something that remained nameless. Whatever it was, it was kept at a distance; we were safe, cocooned in our moral principles.

What war meant and could bequeath reached me only in the most indirect, sketchy ways. My seventh-grade science teacher was a slim, dapper white-haired man with a pinkish complexion and very sharp features that appeared always on the alert, like a fox. Maybe because of his apprehensive look, or because it was true, or for no reason at all, the gossip circulated that he had been shell-shocked in the war. What *shell-shocked* meant, or which war, no one knew or cared. Any sudden loud noise, it was rumored, would send him scurrying under a desk for shelter. The class lived in eager anticipation of this scene, and some students took to dropping books or slamming doors in the hope of provoking it. I was curious too—school was so numbingly dull that any drama would have been welcome—but full of dread. I knew I would have to turn away if it happened, because I have never been able to watch public humiliation. But he never did scurry under a desk, no matter how many books were dropped, so I never got to see even this meager evidence of what war could do.

At the same time that I was taught to believe in human benevolence, striving and progress, that people were basically good at heart, as Anne Frank famously and mistakenly wrote, that virtue would be rewarded but in any case should be practiced for its own sake, and that if everyone obeyed the Golden Rule, all would be well (in school, every classroom had a poster displaying the Golden Rule)—at the same time, the Nuremburg trials were going on. I didn't know about them; I never heard any adult mention them. I don't know when I became aware of them, maybe not until I saw the movie with Maximilian Schell and Montgomery Clift. Montgomery Clift played a victim who had been castrated, which seemed to have affected his mind as well as his body. He couldn't summon the words to say what had been done to him, but I figured it out. I still remember his halting testimony on the screen, and the roiling it worked up in my gut. It was inconceivable that such things could happen. That people could do such things to one another. And this not even in the ancient days of chariots and gladiators I knew about from books. Not even so long ago.

I don't imagine that past generations of American children were burdened with such innocence. Without any public pretense of progress and decency, they couldn't have helped but notice early on that human beings can be bestial, though some are more bestial than others. Surely today's children, wedded to television and video games, cannot remain innocent. And for all I know, my experience, that is, my ignorance, was typical only of my neighborhood, my schools, my family. Every family, after all, is its own minuscule, distorted reflection of the culture at large. But even if other children knew more, those with fathers and brothers returning or not returning from the war, those with mothers working in wartime industries, the public optimism and euphemisms were pervasive.

And short-lived. My own children, born in the 1960s, were knowing early on, even ironic, about the human bent for violence and destruction. They knew there was a war winding down in Vietnam and they knew about the assassinations that had taken place in their infancy, and not only because I told them. It was impossible not to know. The 1960s, which were really the late 1960s and the 1970s, are maligned now, as if all the ruckus was simply drugs and sex and adolescent rebellion, but that is bad press, the opposite of whitewashing. One of the pleasures of the 1960s was their no-holds-barred truth-telling; more truth was spoken in public during those years than ever since, and the truth-tellers were loud.

There were loud words spoken in my household too, and often truthful ones. While my mother was being good and preaching goodness, my father stomped through our small, cozy rooms shouting his bitter views: that religion was the opiate of the people, that altruism was the mask of self-interest, that the Marshall Plan was not so much generosity as a way of insuring eventual markets for American goods. "Markets, markets, it's all markets," he sputtered, waving his arms in the air and making the venetian blinds and the knick-knacks on the mantel tremble. Yet loud as he was, he couldn't shake my mother's quieter belief in the triumph of moral benevolence. And she was the more reliable guide to the zeitgeist.

I think I didn't take my father's views seriously because they were expressed with such vehemence; there was a quality of parody to his rages, and if they hadn't been so frightening they might have been comic. Their over-the-top volume spoiled whatever force of truth they might bear. It was a kind of preview of what happened with the 1960s, although my father could hardly approve of the countercultural antics. Still, the pattern was the same: if you don't like the messenger's style, just dismiss the message. But a calm demeanor doesn't guarantee reliability; some screamers are screaming truth.

I started school after the war was over. Captivity. The walls of the prison house closing in. That any school was a wretched place to spend one's childhood, I grasped from the first day. In the mornings, each class of about thirty had to form a double line in the concrete, fenced-in school yard, holding hands with our partners, sweaty in spring, mittened in winter. The lines had to be kept straight, and no talking was allowed. We were supervised and silenced by older children called guards (their real title was *guides*, but we always called them guards). The guards wore white bands diagonally across their chests to show their status. The captain of the guards was a sixth-grade boy, the only black child in the school. Later on, in junior high and high school, there were a few black kids among us and they blended in, but I never went to their houses and only once invited a black girl to mine. Racial tension was beyond neighborhood boundaries, out of sight. The black people we saw were maids who came once a week to scrub, then conveniently disappeared, back to their unknown regions, about which no curiosity was ever voiced. It wouldn't be until the mid-1950s that the people on our block would notice that the maids and their families were not entirely contented with their lot.

In fact, curiosity about anything, curiosity as a character trait, was faintly mocked at home, as were travel and adventure. Curious probing would let in information, knowledge that might threaten received wisdom. Every time my wanderlusting uncle took off on another trip to some exotic-sounding place, my mother would shake her head and chuckle, as if to say, Why on earth would anyone bother? I liked that word, *exotic*. I would ask my mother to cook something exotic for dinner, or implore that we go somewhere exotic on vacation rather than to the stultifying mountains, until *exotic* became a household joke, as if my hankering were both quaint and foolish.

School, at any rate, was anything but exotic or adventurous. At the clang of a bell, we were allowed into the classroom, where the regimentation continued, everything done in unison, in silence, in perfect order. Why did we have to line up, anyway? We weren't attending a military academy, just an ordinary public school in an ordinary lower-to-middle-class neighborhood. Why couldn't we stand around in spontaneous clumps? For the convenience of the authorities, so they could keep track of us more easily. Why couldn't we speak? To teach discipline, I suppose, because from discipline sprang order and all good things. One junior high school teacher forbade the opening and closing of the metal rings in loose-leaf notebooks. Random clicking created noise, noise led to disorder, and disorder led to communism.

If we heard virtually nothing of the recent war, we did hear a lot about communism. Communism—or rather anticommunism— came along to fill the space in the collective brain that should have been occupied by pondering the war, its origins, its meaning. Teaching

us to hate communism replaced teaching about the methodical exter-
mination of millions of people, or that there had been a war at all.
A similar displacement, in quite different circumstances, happened
after the 2001 attack on our country. There was little public effort
to examine its historical causes. As long as we have an undisputed
and fanatical villain to blame, further thought gets shut down. To
understand forces at work larger than Osama bin Laden or Al Qaeda
doesn't grip our imaginations or engage our energies. What enlivens
us instead are fears and threats. Just as I was trained to crouch under
my school desk in case of a nuclear attack by the Russians, today we
deepen the color of the terrorist threat—yellow to orange to red.
Moral righteousness calls the tune, and fright is the beat we dance to.

Miss Koslowski, the seventh-grade history teacher, was hunch-
backed, tiny, and embittered, the terror of junior high. She was
famous for making strong boys weep if they hadn't done the homework or forgot the reasons for the Boxer Rebellion. In method and
sensibility she was a Stalinist through and through, who would stride
up and down the five rows of desks kicking any feet that were sticking
out in the aisles. But regardless of her Stalinist sensibilities, her ideol-
ogy was fiercely anticommunist; her warmest words were reserved for
Alexander Kerensky.

Miss Koslowski's pedagogical strategy—and in this she was
emblematic of the times—was to reduce all complexity to outline
form. Three reasons for British imperialism, and three subreasons for
each reason. Three reasons for the Sino-Japanese war. Three reasons
for World War I. History, according to Miss Koslowski, had been
considerate enough to arrange itself in an easily parsable network
of reasons, and if we simply memorized the outlines and categories,
our understanding would be complete. Unraveling that notion took
quite some time.

For the five months I spent in her classroom, I lived in dread, a
miasma of the soul. I always kept my feet out of the aisles and did my

homework in neat outline form and was prepared to answer any and all questions in case I was called on, to avoid the mortification Miss Koslowski inflicted daily. Each night before I went to bed I crossed off the day on a calendar I kept in a night-table drawer and counted how many of my days remained in her classroom. It was a secret misery. I never—none of us ever—thought of complaining to our parents or to anyone at school. We accepted without question that we must endure whatever school imposed on us. Collective action or rebellion was inconceivable, which is probably why I feel sympathetic to the student rebels of 1968. I would have gladly have joined them on the barricades, but I was recently out of school and having babies at the time. I wish it had occurred to me in junior high school to refuse and resist. But acquiescence to authority had the force of learned routine. It was like brushing your teeth; you simply had to do it.

I think another reason we kept silent about Miss Koslowski and similar petty school sadists was to protect our parents. (In my case, my mother. My father knew plenty about sadism: he'd spent his first eleven years as a Jew in a small town near Kiev. But for that very reason he would have dismissed the minor barbarities of Miss Koslowski.) We were hesitant to shatter the idea of the benevolent universe they were trying so valiantly to foist on us. We were being kind, bearing the burden ourselves.

Something else I never told: I was thirteen, crossing a street near home just after dark, when a boy my age or younger suddenly appeared in the dim light and grabbed my left breast. He squeezed and let go and hurried away. I was so startled that I didn't even speak. The whole thing didn't take five seconds. It is taking far longer to write about it. I wasn't frightened. He disappeared before I could feel any fright. Before I could even think, he was gone into the gathering night. Besides, what did I know to fear? Nothing ever happened in our little neighborhood. There was no one more dangerous on the streets than the toothless old woman—the witch, we called her—

from the shabby end of the block; she kept chickens and glared when we rode by on our bikes (any passing cars kindly slowing down). We walked around at all hours and never got mugged; I didn't know what mugging was.

What I was, was stunned. Why would anyone do that? What could impel him? It wasn't like the boys at dimly lit parties trying to inch their fingers towards a breast. I understood that. But this? The only pleasure he could find in his act was the pleasure of startling and distressing me. I had no notion of sexual politics back then, so the fact that I was a girl alone on the street didn't enter into my thinking. What stunned me was the gratuitousness of it, that someone would choose to cause pain and shock in a total stranger.

I didn't suffer any physical harm, only the insult. And beyond that, the affront to my notion of what could happen in my safe, familiar backwater. It was like a match struck in the dark, murky pit of human motivation, just long enough to show a darkness, not long enough to illuminate it. It was one of the great shocks of my life, not of course the act itself but the sheer surprise. Of course it's nothing compared to what I've known and witnessed since, to what I read in the papers every day. As we used to say in Brooklyn, that should be the least of my troubles. When I recall it, I no longer feel insulted; his act seems ridiculous. But I do recall it. And I still feel a residue of shock. It was a baffling bit of aggression for which my childhood in America left me totally unequipped.

Years later I learned that everyone in my neighborhood, even my innocent-seeming mother, knew and did all sorts of things I would never have dreamed possible. Mr. K., two houses to the right of ours, beat his wife; she sometimes screamed from the upstairs bedroom window, but when she walked out and greeted the neighbors she was super genteel, the most ladylike of all the local ladies. The father of a friend of mine, Mr. B., a buildings inspector married to a schoolteacher, was being investigated for bribes and kickbacks; that explained why he was home from work so much of the time. Dr. S., a podiatrist and father of another friend, lived half-time with his secretary. I had once gone to his nearby office—also her apartment—and met the scarlet woman. That explained why Dr. S. was so rarely home for dinner. Rumor had it that Dr. G. had performed an abortion on his late wife and inadvertently killed her. One of my cousins married a woman who at age eighteen had eloped with someone highly unsuitable—I never found out in what way. She was damaged goods, but the family generously overlooked that brief escapade and turned out in force for the wedding. Long ago one of my mother's cousins had run over a pedestrian while driving; this explained why his wife always drove, in those days an unusual practice. And on and on.

I found these stories delectable, better than what I read in books because they were true. My mother and older sister would drop them into conversation offhandedly, as if I'd surely figured them out by that time. Hearing them, I felt I'd had a deprived youth. As if there were a whole range of colors or musical notes I'd never been aware of, some of them ugly but all of them exciting, opening up vistas of possibility.

The urge to blame someone or something for my deprivation is very strong. Blaming was a strategy I grew up with; it went hand in hand with the faith in human decency. Blaming was a comfort, and comfort was high on our scale of values. For the older generation, which had endured the war, having a clear villain to blame—Hitler and the Germans—was so satisfying that this brand of comfort became irresistible, addictive. If villains could be found to blame for everything, then evil could be localized and kept in check, like an epidemic. Decent people could remain immune, not just from corruption but from thought.

But who can be blamed for one's own innocence? The spread of illusions about human nature (that it is benign) and human possibility (that it is small) was not deliberate or ill-intentioned; those who fooled me were fooling themselves as well. I can hardly blame a whole era, either. Others of my age caught on faster to what we are and do. The evidence was everywhere, for those with eyes to see.

I can conclude only that some people are born with a tendency to innocence, like a tropism. Or a caul over the eye, the mind. Every day, I rip off the caul, or it's ripped off by the morning news—the war, the tortures, corporate theft, government lies on one side and pusillanimity on the other, the litany that accompanies the first cup of coffee. Every night, as I sleep and dream, the caul creeps back, like a bad habit. I don't prize innocence, yet it clings to me. I don't want to believe I could do the things I read about in the papers, even under extreme pressure. If nothing human is alien to me, then maybe I don't want to be human. A dead-end notion if ever there was one.

In the end, the need to believe in human decency is too deeply buried to be unearthed, too tightly knotted in my history to unravel. If it has any use at all, it is to keep me in a perpetual state of wonder. And wonder makes for writing, which is one way of redeeming our failures. If not effective, it's at least clarifying. Consoling.

Carlos Saura's Cria!

Whenever *Cria!*, the 1976 movie directed by Carlos Saura, is shown in my vicinity, I have to see it. This doesn't happen very often. Saura has been one of Spain's most prolific and admired filmmakers for nearly half a century, but in this country, he hasn't had the popular success of his mentor, Luis Buñuel, or younger compatriot, Pedro Almodóvar. Not long ago, though, *Cria!* was shown in New York City along with some two dozen of Saura's more than forty films, so naturally I went.

There are only a handful of movies I've felt compelled to see more than once, and what keeps me coming back are the most flagrantly obvious moments. In the realms of literature and music I may be an educated consumer, but when it comes to films, my tastes don't run to the subtle. *The Third Man*, for the way Alida Valli, at the very end, turns her back on nerdy Joseph Cotton and walks down the road from the cemetery, alone and haughty. *The Prize*, one of the all-time great bad movies, for the mistaken-identity ploy that has Edward G. Robinson croaking, with his last breath, "But I'm an actor! Only an actor!"

With *Cria!*, a brooding yet exhilarating family drama set at the end of the Franco era, it's nothing so specific. If I had to choose one scene, it would be the three sisters, recently orphaned, dancing in their bedroom in a well-appointed, gloomy house in the middle of Madrid. Their dancing goes on for quite a while; Saura loves dancing of all kinds and did a documentary devoted to flamenco. I wouldn't mind if it went on for hours. It's that magical—for me, an enduring image through which the rest of the film is refracted. This time, when I saw *Cria!*, I wanted to deconstruct its spell.

What entrances is not only the music, the Spanish pop tune "Porque te vas," about love and loss, plaintive yet lively. I can hear it in my head as I write. Nor is it the dancing itself, though the girls are beautiful to watch, each in her own way. Irene, the oldest, around twelve, in her jeans and tight shirt already shows intimations of a woman's body, and her swaying gestures verge on the sexy, yet she's still a child. Slender Ana, the protagonist (played by Ana Torrent) and middle girl, about eight or nine, moves like a twig in a faint breeze, her face an enigma, partly amused, preternaturally wise. Maite, about five, has the round stomach and rooted stance of early childhood; her face is jolly and serene and her body bounces with enthusiasm as she imitates what her big sisters do.

The particular allure is not tangible but rather subtle and pervasive, like a nuance of light or aroma. It's the feel of the sisters' unity, the unquestioned solidarity and love that keeps them dancing, and together, their persistent exuberance in spite of the emotional cruelty and stagnation they've witnessed. We get an inkling of just how much they know when, after both parents are dead, the girls dress up in their clothing and act out scenes of the marriage. Irene, in wig and mustache, plays the husband, and Ana the wife; suppressing mischievous grins, they mimic to perfection the dialogue of accusation and defense, rising hysteria against grim withdrawal, culminating in, "But the children, the children will hear you!" Even in this parody, the redemptive quality of the girls' love—and cleverness—overcomes the nastiness.

Judging from other films—*Ana and the Wolves, Mama Turns 100, Garden of Delights*—Saura's view of the family is not benign. Generosity and loyalty are the exception; more often the prevailing ambience is indifference, resentment, envy or worse. *Cria!* shows a marriage in a state of decay, the wife disappointed, frayed by misery and illness and finally dying in agony; the husband a rigid, unprincipled army man, habitually unfaithful, impatient with his wife's tears and recriminations. The ossified marriage, like many of the bleak or corrupt situations Saura chooses, seems an oblique comment on the Franco regime.

Like his other films, *Cria!* is emotionally charged, but while it offers the ingredients of high drama—seduction, betrayal, passion, strife, illness, death—it doesn't hold the viewer by anything so commonplace as plot. What we follow is less a narrative unfolding than characters responding erratically to circumstances and creating new circumstances in turn. That is, like life itself: plotless but dense with events. Right at the outset, the burdens of memory and death announce themselves with a montage of family photos showing the recently deceased mother, played by Geraldine Chaplin, in happier days.

In the very first scene, Ana prowls through the house at night, her face impassive, arresting. In her high-waisted, long white nightgown, she might have stepped out of a Velasquez painting, maybe *Las Meninas*. Descending the heavy, curved staircase, she hears moans of passion from her father's room. Then the moaning changes, becomes frantic gasps for breath. A terrified woman, hastily buttoning her dress, rushes from the room and out the door without acknowledging Ana, who stands silent in the darkened living room, apparently unmoved, even unsurprised, by what she soon understands is her father's sudden death (later we'll understand why there's no surprise).

His funeral is stern and lugubrious, a sharp contrast to the children's colorful bedroom: stiff uniformed men line the windowless room as the girls are brought, one by one, to kiss the lips of the corpse.

Ana, who blames her father for her mother's misery and fatal illness, is the one who refuses: "I don't want to," she says, shocking the assembled company.

The story takes place during a school vacation, though it slides effortlessly from present to past and back. With both parents gone, the children are cared for by a well-meaning but officious aunt and an outspoken, devoted housekeeper. Mostly they care for themselves, ambling about the walled-in garden with its empty swimming pool—a big blue abyss—or playing in their room. Saura respects the sobriety of children's play. Ana tends to her guinea pig. Irene cuts out pictures from fashion magazines for a scrapbook and enlists the tiny Maite to help as best she can: to each according to her needs, from each according to her abilities.

Out of their isolation, they make a utopian family. The dancing and games in the bedroom evoke a peaceable kingdom, *L'isle joyeuse* of legend. It's the lush super-reality, I think, that keeps me returning—to see an illusion made visible, a buried dream of prelapsarian harmony, a perfect mutual understanding none of us has ever known, only dreamed of.

Death, a palpable presence in the house, seeps into the girls' games. During a weekend visit to friends in the country, they play hide-and-seek on the lawn. In their version, when Ana discovers her sisters' hiding places, they are supposed to die. "Die!" she commands. Maite collapses in one piece onto the grass; Irene enacts a slow, mock-romantic death, clutching her chest and swooning. The next step is for Ana to revive them. She chants an invocation ending with "Bring my sisters Irene and Maite back to life," at which they spring up happy and intact. After so much real loss, the game's wry subtext is, Death, where is thy sting?

The hide-and-seek ritual signifies more than play. Ana believes she has supernatural powers that go even beyond bringing back the dead.

. . .

Using children as protagonists is a delicate venture. Saura avoids all the ready pitfalls by taking the girls utterly seriously. They are not cute or marginal or instrumental; they are not patronized, nor do they represent victimhood or sweet potentiality—all the uses to which children are put in adult movies. We don't feel sorry for them, or protective. We're simply mesmerized as the camera lingers on each one caressingly, like the wraithlike mother who smooths Ana's hair over and over, in wrenching scenes where Ana conjures her up, trying, with all the force imagination can summon, to dream her back to life. This stringent but respectful treatment recalls the historian Philippe Aries's approach to childhood in his controversial study, *Centuries of Childhood*. Aries argues that European children in the Middle Ages were regarded as miniature adults who took part in the work and amusements of society, assumed responsibilities and were held accountable for their actions. Only later on did childhood come to be seen as a distinct phase of life, and children regarded as intrinsically other, requiring elaborate civilizing techniques. "In the tenth century, artists were unable to depict a child except as a man on a smaller scale," Aries writes. Just so, Saura depicts the girls as complex beings on a smaller physical scale, as fully realized and subtly textured as the adult characters around them.

. . .

In between Saura's first feature, *Hooligans* (1960), about disaffected, aimless youth and modeled on the Italian postwar realists, and *Iberia* (2005), a series of musical variations on Albeniz's *Iberia Suite*, is a range of exceptional variety—psychological drama, family saga, historical epic, folk tales, an adaptation of Garcia Lorca's *Blood Wedding*, and more. The influence of Buñuel is evident, but beyond that, the films are infused with Saura's distinctive intensity, eccentricity and signature motifs. One of these is extremely thin women, personified by Geraldine Chaplin, who was his muse and partner for ten years and appears in a number of the films. In *Cria!* she plays the mother, as well as Ana grown up, her bony face filling the screen at intervals, reflecting on her story. For *The Seventh Day*, a tale of rural feuding that ends in carnage and devastation, made some thirty years later, Saura found a very young actress equally gaunt and used her in exactly the same way.

A recurring image is grim, stately, isolated houses, each with a messy junk room piled with broken furniture, obsolete machinery, outworn paraphernalia, trunks of old clothes that the characters try on in ritualized play. The junk room is like the id of the solid bourgeois household, or perhaps its unconscious, a repository of shards of memory, forgotten fragments that represent swathes of history.

Wheelchairs appear frequently, emblems of paralysis and impotence, another comment on the censorious regime Saura had to keep in mind as he worked. The surreal closing scene of *Garden of Delights* (1970), one of the most politically explicit of his films, shows all the main characters in wheelchairs, tooling about their spacious, arid garden. (The Spanish government wouldn't allow *Garden of Delights* to be screened for the Cannes, Berlin and Venice festivals.)

Photos, emblematic of memory, are ubiquitous. Besides ordinary family snapshots, we see doctors' X-rays, home movies, clippings from fashion magazines. Indeed Saura revels in all kinds of artifacts and artifice. When the middle-aged protagonist of *Garden of Delights* suffers amnesia after an auto accident, his father attempts a "cure" by restaging key events from his past. The patient, in his wheelchair, is forced to relive each early trauma, beginning at the age of five, when his mother punished him by putting him in a dark room with a pig. For this purpose, a pig is trotted into the drawing room: this is Saura at his most eccentric. (Aries's remark about childhood, in this context, is turned upside down, as Saura depicts the man as a child on a larger scale. The excruciating scene suggests that we carry early traumas forever in their original incarnation and intensity. The adult crying and cringing at the sight of a pig bares the hidden secret, the self revealed like a negative yielding up its contours in a darkroom.)

Women are constantly observed at the labor of artifice—styling their hair, putting on makeup. (In *Cria!*, an early scene lingers on the girls being dressed and groomed for their father's funeral.) A scene of a middle-aged woman patiently teasing her hair might serve as a lesson for hairdressing students. My favorite is a woman being taught to put on false eyelashes: once they're in place, she learns, the lashes must be separated with a pin. *Peppermint Frappe*, a sinister film from 1967, relies on an elaborate makeover, as an obsessed doctor transforms his meek, dark-haired nurse into the woman he loves—a cavorting blonde sprite in miniskirts. In Buñuel-like fashion, the doctor forces reality to fit his fantasies. Actually, the transformation is not as challenging as it might seem, since both roles are played by Geraldine Chaplin.

■ ■ ■

In works grounded in psychology and realism, *Little Women*, for instance, or worldly social novels, those by Alice Adams, for example, the sisters or friends often number four. Four serves to highlight selected traits, each magnified in a single character, each leading down different paths to different destinies. Three is dense with history and allusion, evoking a more ancient, solemn mood. The Greek Furies who exact vengeance are three, as are the Graces. Not that Saura had Greek myths in mind when making *Cria!* Rather, the film brings myth to mind: the gravity with which the camera hovers over the girls' faces gives their features and expressions a weight of allusion, the portent of symbol.

In three-sister stories, similarities trump differences. What matters is that the three undergo the same circumstances, though their responses may vary, as with Chekhov's three sisters, languishing in the country and dreaming of Moscow, or the sisters in *King Lear*. The sisters in *Cria!* endure the same events. Yet while the main story is Ana's—her inscrutable face is rarely off the screen—Saura grants the fullness of autonomy to each. He gives the last word to Irene, who tells Ana a dream she had of being kidnapped and locked in a room. When the kidnappers phoned her parents to ask for ransom money, no one answered. Just as they were about to shoot her, she woke up. It's a dream that mingles pubescent fantasies with the anxieties of an orphaned child. It's also Saura's way of saying that each girl will bear into the future her own construct of these grief-stricken weeks.

The most ancient triad is the three fates of Greek mythology: Clotho, who spins the thread of life, Lachesis, who measures its length, and Atropos, who snips it. Ana fancies herself a kind of Atropos. She believes she has power over life and death through a secret treasure—a small can containing a deadly poison. One teaspoon could kill an elephant, her mother once told her with mock horror, so throw it in the garbage right away. But Ana took her words literally and kept the can (actually harmless bicarbonate of soda) in a basement junk room near the empty swimming pool. It is this "poison" that she deliberately puts in her father's bedtime drink the night he dies of a heart attack.

Flush with the delusion of success, she offers it to her grandmother, mute in her wheelchair, whose only diversion is gazing at old family photos. "Do you want to die?" Ana asks her kindly. "I can help you." At first the grandmother nods, then changes her mind with a poignantly indifferent shrug, as if it hardly matters. Or, why bother? Ana's final toying with the threads of life comes when she puts the powder in her aunt's milk, hoping to be rid of her inept stabs at child rearing. The next morning brings a jolt when Aunt Paulina appears, as alive and irritating as ever.

Ana's playing so nonchalantly with death does not taint the

dream of ideal harmony evoked by the sisters' dancing. That dream has nothing to do with innocence, which is so glibly associated with childhood. Even aside from the "poison," the sisters certainly aren't innocent, given the ugliness they've seen. I would never be moved or attracted by innocence in any case. Not after my growing up in an era of false innocence. The guiding myth of the postwar Eisenhower years was that decency had definitively triumphed over evil. Parents tried to shield their children, and themselves too, from what they had just lived through. People were basically good, we were taught, or at least educable. If they behaved badly, their education must be at fault. Only much later did I grasp how misguided and dangerously misleading those myths were.

I haven't a grain of nostalgia for lost innocence; the idea is usually specious to begin with. But the vision of benign human nature that accompanies it dies hard. *Cria!* is irresistible because it makes that cherished misconception tangible, in the form of the sisters in their private idyll. That idyll also shows the tireless exuberance of childhood, when grief was always intermittent and sorrow could be lightened by a pop tune or a game of hide-and-seek. Because it has the heartbreak of a splendid illusion, I can watch it again and again, and always, it vanishes when I step back into daylight. With this particular illusion, probably that's for the best.

The morning that shows Aunt Paulina alive and well after drinking the "poison" ends Ana's illusion about her supernatural powers. It also ends the vacation: it's time for the girls to put on their school uniforms, leave the walled-in house and garden and take their place in the world. In the closing scene, set to the same bouncy melancholy song that has played throughout, they join the crowd on the busy Madrid street and make their way to school. It's an image of freedom—escape from the stifling house and its memories of death—but also of conformity. They join a stream of girls in identical uniforms, all headed for the imposing building and the regimentation of class.

Cria! was released to a Spain transformed after Franco's death. Perhaps the girls streaming into the school represent more of Saura's wry skepticism: hope for a new generation brought up in freedom, along with the suspicion that no matter what the politics, after vacation, childhood will always be constricted by uniforms and walls.

Ultimate Peek-a-boo

From day one, she stares right at us. We flatter ourselves by thinking, Already she's interested in us! But the books say that an infant can barely distinguish faces from the pictures on the walls or the furniture. We persevere, stay nearby so she'll know us. When she does start to distinguish faces from the pictures on the walls and the furniture, we want our face to be one of the important ones. (After her parents, of course. No envy or rivalry there. We know what their love feels like, that love fraught and agitated, doused in anxiety.) Soon she distinguishes us, for sure. She's happy to see us. When we appear at the door, she has an inkling of what to expect. Because when we're left alone with her, we let her see our intimate face. We hide our face in our hands, then show it. Look, I'm here. Now I'm not here. Here, not here. And she laughs uproariously.

We talk to her in our intimate voice. We sing to her. And we discover that she's musical: a born music-lover, like us. She looks nothing like us, though she has a quarter of our genes, but she has the music. We sing to her with our best, our secret, voice, a voice dense with emotion that we're shy about showing the others, on the rare occasions when we do sing in front of others. And she loves our singing, as no one else in the world does—there's no reason why they should. We sing and she listens, rapt. It started, this singing, as a way to quiet her when she was fretful, but soon it became our private thing, what we do together. When she can stand up, she dances. We find music with a strong beat and she bounces up and down, little ballet pliés. Over the years, we've often danced alone in the kitchen, holding a mixing spoon, and now we have someone to dance those silly dances with.

Now when we appear she looks at us the way no one does anymore, and maybe no one ever will again: Oh, it's you. You intrigue me. Singing, music. I want to know all about you. What else is there, her eyes (gray, green, blue?) ask, besides the music?

Well, I've got a few other things up my sleeve, but she's not quite old enough. I'll wait until she's ready—as long as I can, at any rate. I used to think at this point I wouldn't learn much more, anything truly new, that is. Not so. She's something I don't know at all, something left to discover. As she discovers me. Together we're engaged in an endlessly intriguing mutual scrutiny. And while we're at it, I'm winning her confidence, so if she ever hears the music of the spheres, she'll tell me what that sounds like.

Being a grandmother. What to say about a subject so strewn with cliché and sentimentality that it's as daunting as a minefield? I once heard the writer Grace Paley tell a group of students that the old saw "Write what you know" was too simple-minded. Rather, write what you don't know about what you know. She was right. There's no thrill at all in setting down what we already know, or only an accountant's thrill, a cartographer's thrill. For instance, that the granddaughter is perfection, the most remarkable child that ever lived, and so on. However true, there's nothing there to discover. And to write is to discover.

When the platitudes are swept aside—the freedom from responsibility, from the need to discipline, to civilize—we're left with a peculiar late-life love affair. To understand its potency, you have to ponder love affairs in general, because this one is similar in its inner dynamics, even if the love object is a fraction of your body weight and can't yet converse, let alone eat properly. The kind of love this new one most resembles is that most universal and best-documented of genres, teen love: the same giddy absorption, the same loss of all sense of proportion, the same transcendent idiocy, when a mere glance from the beloved in the school cafeteria could send us into fluttery spasms. Anything more emphatic brought rampant joy—until the inevitable crash.

I never longed to take that high ride again: to tell the truth, I'd never enjoyed it all that much. I'm not a sucker for romanticism, and I'd rather be mildly tipsy than blind drunk. Fortunately this reincarnation of crazy love offers the adoration without the agony, which was tangy, certainly, but toxic.

All that, though, is the known part. Beyond the known is a state of being that's mysterious and unsentimental, even a bit scary in its utter irrationality. There's something suspiciously viral about the condition: relentless, forceful and all-consuming. Those it strikes feel helpless, stupefied, even stupid in their immersion. Before it struck me, I'd listened—patiently, indulgently—to others in their blithe affliction. I'd never be susceptible, I thought. I knew love—infatuation, passion, devotion, the whole business—inside and out; I wrote the book—lots of them, actually—about the ways we link or entwine or hook up. No variety of attachment could subjugate me.

That was another thing I didn't know.

The love grandparents bear for their grandchildren is viewed sentimentally as the purest of passions. But all love affairs have their source in self-love, and this one is no exception. Beneath the selfless grandmotherly devotion, I suspect, lurks the same self-serving quest as always. The allure of love is being seen. Even more, being seen anew. Seen right. Granted, from time to time we may fix on some distant paragon who's blind to us, but the vertiginous plunge doesn't really occur until we find ourselves mirrored in the answering glance. Meaning that we love the person who sends back the most flattering reflection, whose vision of us fits most precisely with our own—cut from the same cloth, and congruent. On more lasting acquaintance, that perfect fit may not endure, just as our most cherished clothes tend to fit less well over time, as the body, that notoriously unstable landscape, shifts and betrays. It might happen that we have to go seeking an entirely new outfit. (Though it won't with the grandchild, I'm quite sure.)

Like so many perturbations of the heart, what makes this one interesting and worth parsing is, precisely, its impurity. The wonder of the grandchild is that she sees us with fresh eyes, granting us that most egotistical of thrills. Eyes that couldn't, indeed, be fresher—they've hardly seen anything else. She's an empty mirror on which we can flash our best self, see it registered and flashed back. A perfect reflection: she doesn't know enough to make judgments or be critical.

Of course, like any newborn creature, the grandchild is not a blank slate. Anyone who's ever observed the visible nuances of heredity knows that; now, with the mapping of the human genome, it's obvious even to those who require scientific proof. But she's blank as regards her impressions of us. In that way, she differs from everyone else in the world, all the people we know who've already formed their impressions and opinions. And we needn't worry about whether she'll love us back. Of course she will. Fresh as she is, she doesn't know enough not to. (In that sense we may be taking advantage of her innocence, but it's a quite benign exploitation.) This, then, is the only relationship where we loved someone infinitely and hadn't a worry in the world about whether they would love us back.

But what about our own children? Didn't we assume they'd love us back? Yes, but that certainty was so clouded over by the dense fears involved in raising them that we couldn't enjoy it with anything like the abandon we feel now. So. Reluctantly, inevitably, we near the tangle shrouding the mystery: to think about grandchildren, we have to think first about children. Immediately, the bright subject flickers and darkens; the plot thickens; complexity looms. Grandchildren are simple; children, not in the least. Ours are grown now and have impressions of us and opinions galore. So many that they've lost interest. Who wouldn't?

Our memories of them as small children are vague, alas, made blotchy by old panics at every stage, panics that blurred our appreciation like smudges on a camera lens. Because it was terrifying, actually, to grasp that they would be forever with us, part of us to death and beyond. It was our job to civilize, socialize them, and what young creatures wouldn't harbor less-than-beneficent feelings for those charged with curbing their appetites and impulses? They thought we were all-powerful. How could they know we were frightened all the while, frightened of them? What would they think of us, how would they judge us, would they ever forgive our civilizing duties and come to love us without reservations? Even more, would they care to know us? Their relation to us was an existential conundrum: we made them, they were our creatures; at times they felt like our possessions. And yet our task was to free them from us. How could we both own them and free them?

For their part, they thought about us both too much and too little. They'd forget us at the oddest times, just when they ought to be remembering us. (Literally—they might disappear overnight and forget to call.) Quite forget our existence, and we'd have to go hunting for them, reminding them who we were and where they belonged. Yet at the same time, they thought about us too much. We're not so important, we wanted to say. Go ahead and do as you like, and stop worrying about what we'll think. We won't think anything. In fact, we'd be very glad to think about ourselves for a change. We fretted over them and they fretted over us, but never at the same times and in the same ways, never in harmony. And sometimes we'd catch each other fretting and send, mutually, a sympathetic, rueful glance of complicity, as if to say, Will we be locked this way forever? Can we free each other?

And then, at some point we did release each other. At some point in young adulthood, they stopped fretting over us, stopped referring to us in their heads at every critical moment. They lost interest and left us behind. And we, who are constitutionally unable to lose interest in them, we, for whom the children are and will be forever a source of fascination because they're ours—and as well as we know them, we still can't predict what they'll do tomorrow—we must paradoxically rejoice that they've outgrown us. We must accept with good grace that we're no longer objects of any interest. We're what they've put behind them. We're simply too well known. There are ways, to be sure, that children don't know their parents at all. But in the long run, those ways don't matter. In the ways that matter, they know us all too well. They've gotten to the bottom of us, and there isn't any more. They find us predictable.

But to the new one, the grandchild, whom we did not produce and whom we do not in any way possess, we're new. We interest her. And—bittersweet gift of mortality—we won't live long enough for her to get to the bottom of us. Meanwhile, we can inscribe the precise image we want recorded, in perpetuity. We can show the self—our self that no one else would care to see. So we murmur secrets, we sing, we dance. We wait. We assemble our gifts for when she's ready. Some of them are even our own books.

Raising children and writing books. Those are the two endeavors we spent our life on. They were our education and our striving after . . . what to call it? Learning to make a livable place for ourselves in the world. Of course there was all the rest of what constitutes a life. There was love, the grown-up kind of love, for one thing. That was an education too, but it was something we learned with another, while the books and the children, when looked at under the aspect of eternity —or as much of eternity as we'll ever know—were what we had to learn, all alone, to master. Many more books than children: children take more time and work. And the two strivings were always in conflict. Always attended by guilt and doubt. Each seemed to detract from the other. When we were writing, we felt it was time we ought to be giving the children. With the children, we felt it was time we ought to be giving the writing. We never figured out a satisfactory balance, and eventually we learned to live with that incessant tug-of-war.

We felt at times, with a gruesome guilt, that if not for the children, we might have written more, and better. At the same time, we grasped that if not for the children, we might not have written anything at all worthwhile; we wouldn't have had anything to write about. Not that we wrote exclusively about child rearing or family life, not at all. What we wrote about perpetually, however varied the books appeared to be, was the evolution of character, what it meant to become and remain a human being; what it felt like, here and now, to be the enigmatic, flawed, mortal, relentlessly self-conscious creatures we are, struggling constantly between the world within and the world without, mediating between what we are and what we yearn to become, what the world will permit us to become. (Come to think of it, we wrote all our lives as we're doing right here, that is, teasing out the slightly disreputable motives beneath the innocuous surface.)

None of this could we ever have understood without the children, without watching their astonishing transformation from know-nothing, frangible infants into something resembling . . . us. In that sense the children gave us our writing life, our raw material, and we should be grateful.

We observed the genetic code unfolding and marshaling its forces, preparing to collide with circumstance and destiny. We gathered our data on what shapes human nature as it undertakes its delicate negotiations with the world, and this ramifying human nature and these worldly transactions became the subject of our work. But we couldn't watch with the kind of thorough and dedicated attention such research deserves, because these were, after all, our children. We had to feed them and clothe them and see that they didn't choke on buttons or put forks in electrical sockets or run out in the street under the wheels of a car. (And when one did run out in the street in front of a car and we ran out to grab her, we realized instantly that the old cliché about mothers is true.)

Which brings another cliché, one of those swept aside earlier, scuttling back to our aid: yes, grandparents are more relaxed, less anxious and burdened, so they can enjoy the grandchild. Except that it's not the enjoyment part that absorbs me. Sure, that giddy, adolescent high is a blessing right up there with the best of life's intoxicants, but being ineffable, it doesn't bear analysis. What does bear analysis is the intense, focused concentration on the process of becoming human, embodied in the grandchild, who metamorphoses into a person right before our eyes, a live documentary in slow motion.

When we point to our hand and she points to hers, right in front of her, that's simple to understand. When we point to our nose or eyes or chin and she points to hers, how does she know? How does she know she has a face that's the same as ours? She's too young to grasp what mirrors are for. When I spoon food into her mouth and she tries in turn to put the spoon in my mouth, how does she know I eat the way she does? How does she know she's one of us and not, say, one of the very plump rabbits her parents keep in a cage in the living room, and who are closer to her size than I? What encoded pattern helps her deduce we're the same, only on a different scale? She must figure out that resemblance trumps size as a criterion of species identity. And then she thinks, I eat, so this bigger version must eat too. Once she gets that straight, her next step is, I laugh, I cry, so she must laugh or cry too. She discovers the concept of our common humanity. A little later, though, she finds that "I want" and "She wants" are not always the same thing; they might be antithetical, and so she's got to fight for what she wants. Yes, we're the same, we share a common humanity, but our interests are not always the same. She grasps the primal flaw of human society already, and she's not even two years old.

These aren't questions that can be answered by experiments with rats and mice. They're not questions that can be answered at all, only lived with and incorporated into our ever-shifting mosaics of who we are and might become. We observe and brood over the givens and then piece them together as imaginatively as we can. This time around, with the grandchild, I observe with no conflict at all. Love and work conjoin. My heart may be in thrall, my spirits buoyant as a teenager's in love, but my head is clear.

Clear enough to wonder, for instance, why she finds hiding and revealing so funny. From quite early on, there was that burst of knowing laughter if I covered my face with my hands, then revealed it. There's the element of surprise, of course. But her life is full of surprises: doors open and people materialize; buttons are pressed and lights go on, music and pictures appear. Nearly everything is a surprise to one so new. Only the hiding and showing is so uproariously funny.

Beyond the question of where a sense of humor comes from, what does she intuit about *here* and *not here*? After all, it is the duality we struggle with from birth to death in countless formulations. Love, work, money; courage, power, ambition and confidence. All these crucial components of our lives have a way of appearing and disappearing—being here and then not here—in baffling, even frightening alternation. The ultimate guise that duality takes on is the *here* of birth and the *not here* of death. Could she have some notion that our game is emblematic of the life process? Is she laughing at the succinctness of the gesture: now I'm here, now I'm not? She can't possibly know that just as she recently arrived out of nothingness to be so vividly *here*, just so, I, merrily making only my face disappear, will in time vanish totally to the *not here*. But I know. Nevertheless, I laugh with her, a laughter tinged with that knowledge, making the game more precious, the time left to play more precious, the laughter itself a kind of whistling in the dark.

Listening to
Anthony Powell

Years ago, working at a temporary job in some godforsaken place, bored and friendless, I spent a while on the phone complaining to an old friend about my plight. When I was finished I paused, hoping for some Delphic utterance about how I might endure until my term came to an end. In the past she had been occasionally oracular. The pause lasted for some time, growing weighty with her anticipated wisdom. Finally she said, "What you need is . . ."

I waited, taut.

"A VCR."

Obviously, this was in the dark ages before Netflix. Like other oracular utterances, my friend's counsel was puzzling, even disappointing at first. But it turned out to be the perfect solution. I remembered it much later when I found myself again working in exile—luckily not bored and friendless this time, but in a place I didn't want to be, in a life that didn't seem my own. By then VCRs were common and my sublet house had one, but I had no time to sit in front of it. I needed something for short, intermittent flights from reality. A colleague mentioned listening to books on tape while pacing the treadmill in the gym. Portable. Controllable. Not yet an iPod, but a step in that direction.

Soon I had in my eager hands tapes of the opening volumes of Anthony Powell's epic twelve-volume novel, *A Dance to the Music of Time*. The entire work took up six boxes of tapes, each box holding some ten to a dozen tapes. It was winter. I trudged through the snow in heavy gear and came home to the warm house, the cat that was part of the sublet deal, and the tapes. When I finished listening to one box, I'd seal it up, drop it in the corner mailbox, and phone an 800 number to order the next.

A Dance to the Music of Time, hailed as a twentieth-century British masterpiece, was something I had always intended to read, but I had been daunted by its Proustian magnitude. I thought I had to wait for some endless summer, like the long-ago summer of my youth that I spent with Proust. Anthony Powell's book turned out to be like Proust in other ways as well: its submission to the rigors and caprices of time, its reliance on memory as a magnetic field, its enormous cast of recurring characters. The comparison has been noted often enough by readers and critics and is alluded to more than once by Powell himself, most memorably when the narrator, serving as an army liaison officer, realizes that the French seaside town where he's quartered for the night is none other than Proust's Balbec:

> I had been standing on the esplanade along which . . . Albertine had strolled into Marcel's life. Through the high windows of the Grand Hotel's dining room . . . was to be seen Saint-Loup, at the same table as Bloch, mendaciously claiming acquaintance with the Swanns.

But even though he capitalizes *Time* much of the time, Powell is a Proust minus the fluid poetry and minus the inimitable soul. Proust made pragmatic, stripped of metaphysics. Or more precisely, the novel is Proustian with the social world in its largest sense—lineage, tradition, the tangled web of relationships—inflated and elevated to occupy the place of the metaphysical. Whether society can be successfully made to occupy this place is one challenge of the enterprise, whose true genre is wry social comedy, frequently edging into satire and burlesque.

Proust or no, *A Dance to the Music of Time* was fine for my purposes. I wanted something to see me through, something I couldn't see the end of. In the very first moments of listening, as I heard the words of the second paragraph (though of course I couldn't know it was the second paragraph), I knew I'd found my salvation:

> For some reason, the sight of snow descending on fire always makes me think of the ancient world, . . . human beings, facing outward like the Seasons, moving hand in hand in intricate measure, stepping slowly, methodically, sometimes a trifle awkwardly, in evolutions that take recognizable shape.

Here was an alternate world in which I could live, and for a long time indeed.

I shouldn't give the impression that those opening paragraphs were what I heard first. No. Presumably to ensure that the listener misses nothing a reader would be privy to, the producers of the tapes were excruciatingly thorough. The reading opens with a recitation of the copyright page, followed by the jacket copy, even the blurbs. When opening a book, I find this material a nice apéritif; when listening, it's a delay, like an actor clearing his throat before the great soliloquy. It also has a greater influence than it should, read in the same voice and tone as the text itself. I tend to read jacket copy in a skeptical mood. "The most important fiction since the war," says Kingsley Amis? We'll see about that!

Powell's gargantuan and hugely funny novel is narrated in the first person by Nicholas Jenkins, himself a novelist, who begins as a late-adolescent British schoolboy and progresses through the twelve volumes to early old age; it sweeps through the century from World War I to the antics of the 1960s and 1970s, chronicling the strivings and connivings of a generation bent on making its mark. Meanwhile the old order collapses to be replaced by a new kind of anarchic, aggressive pluralism, many of whose manifestations—student activism, bizarre utopian cults and shoddy clothes among them—the author clearly finds appalling. In fact, I learned later, Anthony Powell was a lifelong Tory and an admirer of Margaret Thatcher. Also, one of his passionate interests was genealogy, which is not surprising given his patient tracings of the histories and labyrinthine connections of invented families that go back centuries, in a few cases to the time of the Norman conquest.

A Dance to the Music of Time sweeps across social classes too, as Nick Jenkins moves through archetypal institutions like the public school (Eton), the university (Oxford) and the army, and through London literary and social circles where the aristocracy, politicians, artists, lowlifes and theatrical types mingle with more ease than one might expect. Powell's life seems in broad outlines to have followed the same paths as his narrator's, and like Jenkins, he was acquainted with the major literary figures of his day. In fact, to informed British readers the novel is doubtless a *roman à clef*, but on this side of the Atlantic and far from home besides, I was not in possession of the *clef*, nor did I seek it. My whole desire was to be transported to an imaginary realm that would welcome me without any passkey.

Had I been reading, I would have made the usual effort to distinguish between the narrator and the author, especially in a novel that appears autobiographical to some degree. But listening, I found an intermediate character muddling my efforts, and this character was the reader, identified on the tape as David Case. Since David Case was so proficient and convincing a reader, I couldn't help imagining that he was Anthony Powell himself, or possibly Nicholas Jenkins himself, confiding his gossip to my ear alone. (Gossip, in its most exalted mode, is what I was hearing and relishing. Much of the dialogue consists of characters, by the dozens, reporting on each other's love affairs, marriages and divorces, career moves, war records, all the assorted high jinks of lives fumbling along in a tumultuous century.) Yet paradoxically, Case's skilled reading also established him as a strong presence distinct from author or narrator: the transmitter of the story. Someone new was added to the cozy intimacy of writer and reader—the proverbial third who makes a crowd. And as in any sudden threesome, the positions of the original intimate pair undergo subtle shifts. Where, in the presence of this newcomer, was Anthony Powell? Where was I?

Hearing fiction read aloud by actors, either on tape or in public performance, is a mixed blessing. It would take a heart of stone not to be entertained by their virtuoso displays. Still, I always feel suspicious. Something is being betrayed. We're all having a good time at the expense of . . . what? The words themselves. The actors, by voice and gesture, illustrate the meanings of the words literally, act them out as in a game of charades. On the page, the words neither have nor need any such assistance: they present themselves and we do the rest. Nothing is lost, or added, in translation. Even though performances give color and vivacity to the words—bring them to life, as we say— these translations into another medium are a trifle patronizing, as if the words themselves can't be trusted to deliver the emotion they bear, as if they were mere lifeless nothings before the actors wrapped their vocal cords around them.

Again, had I been reading the book, it would have been my own voice silently taking on the roles: schoolboys and masters, marriageable society girls, business tycoons, military men from privates to generals, innkeepers, servants, musicians, royalty in exile, demimondaines, editors, spiritualists, communist agitators, plus Welshmen

(Powell himself is from an old Welsh family), Europeans and Americans (South and North, from a charming military dictator to a film-making playboy). Of course David Case played them better than I ever could, but they lived in his impeccable and variegated accents, not mine. If reading is simultaneous interpretation, then Case was doing the interpreting for me. Either I accepted his version whole, or did a simultaneous translation of my own, a translation of a translation. But how could I? I had no text, only his voice. I was enjoying a command performance, an unattainable—for me—accuracy of diction; the price was giving up my own voice, the sonic prism of literature.

Now and then I'd wonder in confusion, Would the "real" Nicholas Jenkins sound like this? *A Dance to the Music of Time* is not quite a bildungsroman, certainly no *Éducation Sentimentale*. Even more than the object of our observation, Nick Jenkins is the point from which we observe—at once a character in formation passing before us and the window through which we regard the passing scene. The trouble is that the window is not quite transparent.

At first, Nick Jenkins seems a self-effacing narrator, even ingenuous—or is it disingenuous? In dialogue, Case-as-Jenkins's tones are bland, and reactions to him are temperate, with only a few exceptions giving clues to his nature. "Why are you so stuck up?" the raucous, vulgar agitator Gypsy Jones asks "truculently." "I'm just made that way." "You ought to fight it." "I can't see why." But Powell has such obvious scorn for poor Gypsy Jones that her judgment is not to be trusted. A smug middle-aged do-gooder remarks that Jenkins does not "seem a very serious young man," no doubt because at that early stage, he shows no evidence of what we'd call "career goals," and his conversational style is terse and marked by levity. A canny fortune-teller (the story is spiced by devotees of the occult) says that Nick Jenkins is "thought cold but has deep affections."

Apart from the dialogue, Jenkins poses as the unobtrusive chron-

icler of his ill-fated contemporaries (alcoholic, depressive, compul-
sively womanizing, killed in battle or in the Blitz), with his own ups
and downs mentioned almost as modest afterthoughts. In truth, Jenkins has us firmly in his grasp, calibrating the viewpoint with his unre-
lentingly ironic commentary. At least David Case's cultivated voice
and accent gave every word an ironic edge. (He could sound super-
cilious even while instructing the listener to "slap the cassette smartly
on a hard, flat surface" if the tape should get stuck.) Whole clauses
might have been set in quotation marks; indeed, I can't imagine a
better example of audible quotation marks than Case's description
of a benefit concert for a "good cause." Of course, most British social
novels cohere thanks to irony—that's one reason we read them. Jenkins himself, brooding on "the complexity of writing a novel about
English life," notes that "understatement and irony—in which
all classes of this island converse—upset the normal emphasis of
reported speech."

But just how sarcastic did Powell intend to be? To find out whether
so pungent an irony was built into the novel and not simply part of
David Case's voice and delivery, I would need to read it later on. The
voice itself, while making me laugh and ponder, was also making me
passive, lulling my critical faculties to sleep. For now, though, I had
no choice but to accept the faint sneer rimming the words, an audible
equivalent of the faint sneer on the face of the cat who took to listening along with me.

Besides, it would be most ungrateful to criticize David Case, who
gave his all through countless hours of taping. Which raises a question
that often nagged at me: did he study all twelve volumes first, planning the dozens of accents and voices he would use? I could picture
his text, the dialogue marked with his own private code for the characters, according to social class, gender, age and nationality. Or could
he possibly have read extemporaneously? He'd have to be something
of a genius to manage that, but maybe skilled actors can sight-read as

well as musicians. A rare slip now and then suggested he might have been sight-reading, for instance, when he adjusted the accent midway through a speech or missed the stress of a sentence. But as a rule he was faultless and unstinting. (Was he ever bored? Tickled? When once in a while his voice began on a new pitch, had the recording machine been turned off so he could laugh or grunt?)

In the unlikely event that he read off the cuff, he couldn't have known that the clumsy schoolboy Widmerpool, at first so Uriah Heepish in his creepy false humility, "the embodiment of thankless labour and unsatisfied ambition," would turn out to be a monstrous and dangerous hypocrite. Must David Case have known Widmerpool's future in order to give an accurate reading of his youth? How remarkable, in general, that actors manage to hint at the seeds of the future lurking in the present, while pretending to be as innocent as the audience itself. How unlike actual life, where we don't know where our natures will lead us, yet must play our roles perfectly, and usually do.

As the novel's villain, finally brought grotesquely low, Widmerpool begins as a comic oaf who's frequently the target of projectiles—a ripe banana, a canister of sugar and, in his late years, a can of red paint. He soon becomes chilling, though no less oafish: "an archetypal figure, one of those fabulous monsters that haunt the recesses of the individual imagination, he held an immutable place in my own private mythology." In Jenkins's mythology, Widmerpool represents exorbitant egotism, will unhampered by any semblance of heart, wild ambition and a narrow, bureaucratic intelligence immune to shame, perpetually rising "from the ashes of his own humiliation," rather like Richard Nixon. As an army major and later a member of Parliament with Stalinist leanings, Widmerpool wreaks havoc, destroying lives and provoking a murky international incident. But beyond his mythic aspects, Widmerpool's periodic and unwelcome reappearances in Jenkins's life carry with them the novel's chief and unifying theme:

a rhythmic recurrence that gives shape to the dance of the title, "the repetitive contacts of certain individual souls in the earthly lives of other individual souls."

Eternal return as a strategy for fiction makes *A Dance to the Music of Time* apt for hearing aloud. Everything in the early books is foreshadowing, no detail arbitrary or forgotten. Each hint and anomaly, each nuance of character will blossom into incident, anecdote, drama or disaster, even if it takes two or three or six volumes—or in my case, weeks of listening. The season changed; the snows melted; the cat stared out the window at budding branches instead of icicles. As I changed my heavy coat for a light jacket, characters I remembered from the winter tapes kept reappearing, altered by Time. By the middle volumes, they were even echoing each other exactly as they might in life—those strange reincarnations when a woman met at yesterday's party recalls your algebra teacher, or the new pharmacist moves with the same gestures as a bygone uncle. Jenkins's brother-in-law evokes his old school friend, the languid, doomed Charles Stringham, dead in a Japanese prisoner-of-war camp; the adolescent look-alike daughter of a once-loved woman stirs Jenkins's erotic memory more than the aging woman herself.

I wasn't resting quietly while taking these meaty matters in. No. I listened mornings while I did a half hour of dance exercises, puttered in the kitchen and prepared to set off for work, and then early evenings, again in the kitchen. Normally, when an author is a stylist, I linger over the sentences I like. Aside from his glittery dialogue, Powell's sentences range from juicily aphoristic ("Though love may die, vanity lives on timelessly") to gorgeously baroque. Nick's speech favors brevity, but his narrative style, like Henry James's, often takes lengthy circuits. At their best, such sentences are brilliantly hyperbolic, at their worst merely tendentious. In any event, to linger over passages on tape, athletic feats and prestidigitation were required. I'd be flat on the floor with my feet over my head when something came along that I had to stop and think about: "There is no greater sign of innate misery than a love of teasing." How true. Or some spectacular gossipy or philosophical bit, such as

> Establishing the sequence of inevitable sameness that pursues individual progression through life, Flavia had married another drunk, Harrison F. Wisebite, son of a Minneapolis hardware millionaire, whose jocularity he had inherited with only a minute fragment of a post-depression fortune.

There was nothing for it but to unwind my body, rewind the tape and play the passage again. Over and over this happened, in the middle of stirring a soup, or packing my briefcase or folding laundry. It was vexing to me and perplexing for the cat, who perhaps was caught up in the narrative and resented the interruption. Other times, I'd turn off the tape to stew awhile at some gross generalization, as when Jenkins passes the site of a bombed-out café where he used to meet an old friend, and muses, "In the end most things in life—perhaps all things—turn out to be inappropriate." Or, when a show of paintings by a friend of his youth makes him "think of long forgotten conflicts and compromises between the imagination and the will, reason and feeling, power and sensuality; together with many more specific personal sensations, experienced in the past, of pleasure and pain," how could I not pause to do the same? After two or three hearings, or after a reflective silence, the rhythms of the phrases would be set in my mind as they could not be from ordinary rereading. And it was in David Case's voice, not my own, that these rhythms lived and continue to live in my ear. Eerie.

Daffodils finally popped out all over my neighborhood. I shed my jacket and dug out my sandals. Soon my job was over; time to leave the rented house and return to my life. Sadly, I dropped the last box of tapes in the corner mailbox and packed up. I felt like Nick Jenkins at the close of an unexpectedly intimate talk with a mellow old retired general:

The change in his voice announced that our fantasy life together was over. We had returned to the world of everyday things. Perhaps it would be truer to say that our real life together was over, and we returned to the world of fantasy. Who can say?

Either way, I had had a fine time, the book was majestic and delicious and irritating, but had I actually read it? How much of its majesty and delight and narrow-mindedness was due to the reader, David Case, rather than the author? How much to my own need? Would my responses and judgments be the same had I "really" read it? Did I underestimate, overestimate, grasp the relative weight of things? Get the characters right? The sense and texture? Would it stay with me, or had it literally floated in an ear, soon to drift out the other?

Back home, I got hold of Powell in the flesh, so to speak. I read the twelve volumes in a fever of curiosity, one after the other, a swift two and a half weeks compared with four months of sporadic listening. I wasn't surprised at the rush of familiarity, but it was not the familiarity of rereading. An unfamiliar familiarity. The airy sounds that had been, for me, the book, were collected in one place, tethered to printed words. And speaking of printed words, the first thing that struck my eye was a matter that may seem trivial but in fact was not. Here were the characters, my companions in exile, whose names I had heard daily over a stretch of months lived more intensely in their world than in my own, and I had been misspelling many of them in my mind. Precisely because they were made-up characters, their names were as important a feature of their identity as any other data. Besides, I am a spelling fetishist: the look of words is as crucial as their sound, and misspelled is as jarring as mispronounced.

The florid, ageless fortune-teller who keeps turning up to read palms, tarot cards and the future at large (always correctly, despite Jenkins's skepticism) was not Mrs. "Erdly," as I had been labeling her, but Mrs. Erdleigh. In life, a rose by any other name may smell as sweet, but in fiction a Mrs. Erdly is not the same as Mrs. Erdleigh. My vision of her changed entirely. She became someone to be reckoned with; formerly a trifle ramshackle, she took on dignity. Another transformation struck the racy (and racing buff) Dicky Umfraville, whom I'd been seeing as Umpherville—unaccountably, since David Case's diction was flawless. The delectable comment, "Like many men who have enjoyed a career of more than usual dissipation, he had come to look notably distinguished in middle age," is truer of an Umfraville than an Umpherville. And Jenkins's commanding officer in the army, Roland Gwatkin, a Welsh bank clerk who harbors fantasies of battlefield heroics, was deromanticized by proper spelling. "Gwatkin" is the squat, sad truth about a character whose first name echoes heroes of chivalric times—*La Chanson de Roland* as well as Ariosto's *Orlando Furioso*.

The spelling jolt once passed, the book was the same—yet different. Not as much unadulterated fun. More than a touch melancholic. (Jenkins, as it happens, writes a book about Robert Burton, seventeenth-century author of *The Anatomy of Melancholy*.) Certain characters who had seemed engagingly lightweight on tape took on density and sobriety. Others became more sinister or more outrageous—on tape, sound had tempered them to a less threatening mode. Complex passages—the many descriptions of paintings, the historical analogies—proved more lucid on the page. Dramatic or comic dialogues had shone more brilliantly on tape. Reading took less time, but was more painstaking and precise. At first David Case's voice accompanied me, a simultaneous sound track, but as I read on, it faded, replaced by my own.

Majestic and delicious it all remained, and even more irritating without the mitigating appeal of its reader. Irritating above all in its wholesale contempt for all efforts at liberal political change, a contempt that might reflect Powell's horror at Stalinism, or just plain snobbery and orneriness. Or, to be reluctantly fair, conviction. ("'Conviction,'" as David Case might sarcastically pronounce it.) Powell seems closest to the character who declares, in true Orwellian spirit, "The people who feel they suffer from authority and oppression want to be authoritative and oppressive." (He was well acquainted with Orwell.) Irritating also for the continual cavalier generalizations about women as an alien and troublesome species, some kind of beautiful and necessary, but regrettable, pest.

David Case could be exonerated from adding his own irony. The irony is all Powell's, shielding each page like a scrim. Even the neutrality of Nick Jenkins's conversation, as rendered on tape, was actually a dryness wrought, or wrung out, to the highest degree, an arch, self-protective detachment so suffusing that it comes to be taken for granted, like London fog, maybe. On the page, it's clear that what Jenkins, and presumably Powell, loathes most is hypocrisy and pomposity. What he admires is character, restraint, style and panache— the aristocratic virtues. He rarely finds them among the aristocracy, though; they are distributed democratically, if sparsely.

But "irony, facile or otherwise," Jenkins acknowledges, "can go too far." Even in comedy. With very few exceptions, Powell is unable or unwilling to say anything with a straight face—what newer generations call fear of commitment, in the moral or philosophical sense. This might be acceptable: no one demands earnestness of Swift or Wodehouse. But Powell solicits our allegiance to what is behind the fixed mask of bemused urbanity—an equally fixed piety.

No one could quarrel with what Powell holds sacred, only with his discomfort in presenting it: first, the sufferings, both military and civilian, during World War II. His most sincere passage occurs at a ceremony of General Thanksgiving held in St. Paul's Cathedral at the end of the war, when for a brief moment, after some initial squirming in the toils of cleverness, Jenkins finds a simple statement of feeling manageable:

> The sense of being present at a Great Occasion—for, if this was not a Great Occasion, then what was?—had somehow failed to take adequate shape, to catch on the wing those inner perceptions of a more

exalted sort, evasive by their very nature, at best transient enough but not altogether unknown . . . Perhaps that was because everyone was by now so tired. The country, there could be no doubt, was absolutely worn out. That was the truth of the matter.

Almost as sacred is genuine friendship as opposed to the utilitarian camaraderie of literary and upper-class life. After seeing his dying friend Moreland in the hospital, Jenkins says, "It was . . . the last time I had, with anyone, the sort of talk we used to have together." Finally, married love, at least the kind we must infer Jenkins enjoys with his wife, Isobel, daughter of a large family of eccentric aristocrats. On this theme, restraint nearly catapults to sentimentality, the satirist's lurking danger.

About his devotion to Isobel and about her perfections, Jenkins is reticent to the point of perversity. Before she ever appears, she's called "rather different" and "a bit of a highbrow when she isn't going to nightclubs." Perfect for him, that is. When she turns up, it's love at first sight, on Jenkins's part at least; Isobel's feelings aren't recorded:

> Would it be too explicit, too exaggerated, to say that when I set eyes on Isobel Tolland, I knew at once that I should marry her? . . . It was as if I had known her for many years already; enjoyed happiness with her and suffered sadness. I was conscious of that, as of another life, nostalgically remembered. Then, at that moment, to be compelled to go through all the paraphernalia of introduction, of "getting to know" one another by means of the normal formalities of social life, seemed hardly worth while. We knew one another already; the future was determinate.

Marriage, a miscarriage and an unspecified number of children ensue. (At one point Jenkins alludes to Isobel's having "her" baby; later on he leaves town for an "arrangement about a son going to school." Otherwise his domestic life is discreetly elided—safe from Powell's acidic pen.) Isobel appears maybe eight or ten times over the twelve volumes; her remarks could fit on a couple of pages, and their tone is uncannily close to Jenkins's own—wry, knowing, understated. Of her tastes, her activities, her predilections, we hear nothing but that she has, like Jenkins himself, a "knowledge . . . of obscure or forgotten fiction."

Sketched with such pious reserve, Isobel is a generic, idealized presence; one suspects that her voice, like Cordelia's, is "ever soft, gentle, and low, an excellent thing in woman." How different from the treatment of Jean Templer, with whom Jenkins has an affair in his midtwenties. Nowhere near as perfect as Isobel, Jean is a far more precise character, rich in subtleties and surprises and sex and shrewdly drawn betrayals. The subject of sex does not graze Isobel. Powell must be aware of some great lacuna, for he tries several times to explain it away. When asked about Isobel, Jenkins eludes the question: "It is hard to describe your wife." Elsewhere he resorts to literary casuistry:

> It is doubtful whether an existing marriage can ever be described directly in the first person and convey a sense of reality. Even those writers who suggest some of the substance of married life best, stylize heavily, losing the subtlety of the relationship at the price of a few accurately recorded, but isolated, aspects. To think at all objectively about one's own marriage is impossible. . . . Objectivity is not, of course, everything in writing; but even casting objectivity aside, the difficulties of presenting marriage are inordinate. Its forms are at once so varied, yet so constant, providing a kaleidoscope, the colours of which are always changing, always the same.

A poor excuse from a writer who manages to present, without much worry about objectivity, the broad spectrum of postwar political hues, or the finest nuances of social class, or the changes in attitude towards homosexuality or the psychic toll of alcoholism, depression and thwarted affection. Beyond misplaced piety, the reason for Powell's constraint with Isobel is not hard to fathom: her virtues undermine the novel's presiding view of women as willful items of merchandise passing themselves from one man to another. Even in her absence, Isobel defies one character's view that "the minds of most women are unamusing, unoriginal, determinedly banal." She couldn't possibly be treated as another suggests: "Why discuss your work with her?...Tell her to get on with the washing up." Perhaps she conforms to the type Jenkins describes approvingly as a suitable companion for a writer, "unusually pretty, . . . also to all appearances bright, good-tempered and unambitious." No wonder Powell has more to say about eccentric, foolish, promiscuous and downright awful women than about the classic helpmeet. Dreadful Pamela Flitton, a brittle, preda-tory avenger, is, in literary terms, the best of women, drawn with zest and esprit.

In the end, reading brought no great shocks. I found I had already absorbed the book through the ear and through the pores; I had heard its music, tripped to its rhythms, joined in its dance. Its prejudices I had passed over more easily than I would have on the page, or rather had let them pass over me as I stirred my soup and the tape rolled on. I suspect I might not have loved it so much had I first encountered it in print. Enjoyed, yes, but not loved. Cold, austere and supremely amusing, perfect tonic for my apathy, it is not lovable in the manner of Jane Austen or even Ivy Compton-Burnett. Probably it was the faith-ful performance of David Case that I loved. His role was paramount. And enduring: because of it, I'll never know what I might have felt or thought about the novel as a "mere" book.

Of course, on the page, *A Dance to the Music of Time* is its own grand performance too, exquisitely choreographed and staged with the deep genius of a Balanchine and the deft direction of a Busby Berkeley. And because of the limits of ear and of memory, I couldn't appreciate the grandeur of its design until my marathon weeks of reading.

Powell's dance comes full circle to end where it began. I missed this the first time around. Forgot in May the words that had so enthralled me in January. That early passage, "For some reason, the sight of snow descending on fire always makes me think of the ancient world," refers to a group of workmen huddled around a bucket of flaming coke, taking a break from fixing the pipes beneath a London street as Nick Jenkins happens by. His musings on the ancient world lead him in turn to memories of school, and so the story begins.

At the close of the twelfth volume—I'm only a season older, while Nick Jenkins is nearing seventy—he visits a gallery showing paintings by a long-dead friend. In keeping with Powell's notion of periodic recurrence, the artist who had barely been taken seriously in his own time has been rediscovered as an example of what we'd call "outsider art." On the way, Jenkins notes offhandedly "the street in process of being rebuilt." Afterwards, having seen the paintings (and coincidentally run into his old faithless lover, Jean Templer), he walks out into the starting snow: "The men taking up the road in front of the gallery were preparing to knock off work. Some of them were gathering around their fire-bucket."

The attentive reader is ready to begin all over again, to think again of "the ancient world," and then of school and the long life and long century that followed, "of human beings, facing outward like the Seasons, moving hand in hand in intricate measure, stepping slowly, methodically, sometimes a trifle awkwardly, in evolutions that take recognizable shape."

Reality Tour

When the creaky elevator at last reached the eighth floor, it opened onto another country. Somewhere in Africa, it seemed, although the building was in downtown Manhattan. The dim, narrow lobby was sultry with bodies, mostly men in dashikis and pillbox hats, *kofias*, talking in clumps or navigating their way through the crowd. Facing the elevator was a glass wall, and in the studio on the other side, an African dance class was in progress. Besides the sound of the drums, snatches of French bounced through the lobby, along with an English so accented it might as well have been French. The handful of Americans, black and white, looked like tourists. I felt like a tourist myself, ignorant of the customs of the country. I even felt a twinge of apprehension, as if I might at any moment have to justify my presence, maybe even present my passport.

I could readily justify my presence: I was there to learn to drum. At first I'd felt shy about joining the drum class. What would my fellow drummers make of me, a middle-aged white woman who, however musical, had never been near a drum in her life: this would be obvious right away. What was I doing in their territory? This kind of thinking was foolish, I told myself, and must be overcome. I was paying the fees like everyone else; I was entitled to my adventure.

I made sure to arrive early each week so I could watch the last few minutes of the dance class through the glass. The gray-haired male teacher, wearing loose green and gold trousers and a tunic, would lead the dancers across the floor, sweat spraying from their bodies, arms and legs flinging relentlessly to the beat of the drums. Then they would gather in a circle. A few of the bolder ones came to the center to improvise while the others cheered them on. As they filed out, one by one they thanked the drummers and shook their hands.

I watched with a kind of wistfulness. I had taken dance classes like this one a few years ago. In my old class we used to thank the drummers too, but instead of a formal handshake we each hugged our three drummers. At the beginning I felt hesitant about offering my sweaty body, but the drummers never shrank from us; they happily accepted our tributes, our wet hands and faces. I was entranced by the drums. I listened so closely that sometimes I didn't pay enough attention to the steps and floundered. I was entranced by the drummers too, the way their faces were so somber and concentrated while their hands whirred like oversized hummingbirds' wings.

At some point I got a flu that was hard to shake, and after I recovered I never went back to the class. The prospect of all that leaping around made me limp, as if the flu were reclaiming me. I missed the dancing, but even more, I missed the drums. I could buy CDs, sure, but even better, I could become a drummer myself. Why not? I'd never be more than a so-so dancer, but drumming was something I might have a gift for. I'd played the piano all my life, and when I danced, my timing was impeccable, even if I didn't get the steps right because I was so absorbed by the drums.

Before each week's class, I signed in at a small desk and paid. Fifteen dollars for the class, three dollars to rent a drum, and another dollar, optional, for a bottle of water, a good idea because the drumming was hot work. Some people brought their drums with them, in padded black cases on wheels, but I was renting one. Later, depending on how the classes went, I might buy a drum, though it would be cumbersome to lug it on the subway. The rental drums were kept in a glass cabinet in the lobby. The first few times, I stared at them, not knowing how to choose, until a passing teacher pointed out which would be best for me. I would drag the drum into a very small windowless room with black walls and eight or so ancient folding chairs arranged in a circle. More chairs were stacked against the wall. It was summer and we kept the door closed for the air-conditioning, so it was like playing in a closet filled with pounding rhythms. The closet became a world of pure sound, an isolated capsule of passion in the dark. Everything outside dropped away.

The drum we played was a West African djembe, shaped like a headless woman, a broad-shouldered woman, tapering down to a thin waist and flaring hips that were narrower than the upper torso. We held her, or rather, it, between our legs, not flat on the floor but tipped slightly outward at about a thirty-degree angle, balanced on the outer edge of its round bottom rim. You play a djembe with bare hands. After an hour and a half of slapping the cowhide surface, my hands were hot and stinging. A pleasant sting, the sting of effort.

There were about half a dozen regulars in the class. A thirtyish woman, tall and slim, who took the dance class, came in panting and shiny with sweat, still in her dancing clothes. Another woman had her long blonde hair arranged in African braids as if she were trying to become African. A stocky white man with very dark hair, an accomplished drummer, spoke only French. A young girl, maybe eleven or twelve, would sometimes wander in after the class had begun, take a seat and drum for a while with an absent-minded look, then wander out. New faces turned up occasionally, people who got wind of the place—once two Japanese tourists, once a plump American man who'd been given a djembe as a gift and wanted to learn to use it. Sometimes these people would reappear but most often not.

One by one the students came in, and then came our teacher,

Etienne, glistening from drumming for the dance class. Etienne was in his early twenties, dark-skinned, stocky, of medium height, dressed in jeans and a sweatshirt and a cap pulled low over his eyes. He seemed very sober, almost intimidating, but when he smiled he was transformed, radiant, not intimidating. He greeted the regular students heartily, with a hug and lots of exclamations, in English or French. After I'd come three or four times he started to greet me with a hug and exclamations too, as if I were a long-lost friend he hadn't expected to see so soon again. I liked that: I wanted to be considered one of the regulars. Already I was starting to feel superior to the drop-ins who knew nothing, while I knew something. Not much, but I did catch on quickly and could keep up with the others. I was right, I thought happily: I could get good at this if I persevered.

Etienne began each class by playing a phrase—a pattern of sound—and we would copy it. If we did it accurately he moved on to the next pattern; if not, we had to repeat it over and over until he was satisfied. He never said we were playing well; he just allowed us to continue. There was very little talking altogether. If newcomers were present Etienne might say a bit about how to hold the drum and about the three strokes of the hands: slap, tone, and bass. Slap, a sharp stroke using the heel of the hand and the fingers spread. Tone, with the fingers closed and nearer to the rim. Bass, hitting the center of the drum with the whole hand. Now and then he might come over to position our hands correctly or give instructions in his thick French accent, his manner at once stern and kindly—a stern reverence regarding the proper playing of the drum, but kindly to each individual student. But mostly we learned by listening and copying, and drumming ceaselessly for an hour and a half. Even though I loved to drum, toward the end the sting in my hands made me watch the wall clock, waiting for relief.

At some point during the class a woman from the front desk would appear in the doorway and compare the class list with our small group of drummers, tallying. She might say a word or two to Etienne, but we were so absorbed in our enchanted bubble of sound that we barely noticed her. After a moment or two she would disappear.

We played two rhythms over and over—songs, Etienne called them—for months, learning them phrase by phrase, then putting the phrases together like a collage. Or, in their irregular repetitions, like an auditory mobile. I went home with their rhythms in my hands, and for several days would move my fingers in these rhythms, hearing them in my head and feeling my hands alive and twitching with them. Like a real drummer, I thought: I was becoming a drummer. If I mentioned the class to friends, they responded with a kind of puzzled awe, as if I'd revealed an exotic facet of myself they had never suspected, and this puzzlement and awe gave me a secret delight. It was not surprising to me that I could drum, but it seemed to surprise everyone else. Indeed, telling about my new adventure was no small part of my pleasure in the drum class.

Very soon I realized that the more experienced students, the regulars, were playing more complicated patterns than the beginners, patterns that added texture to the sound the group made. And when we were going along well, Etienne would take off on his own with an even more elaborate riff. His large hands flew so fast above the drum that they became a blur, like the blades of a propeller. Sometimes he would croon along with his drumming, and once or twice he taught us the words to one of the songs and we sang the unfamiliar syllables as we drummed. From time to time another teacher would appear in the doorway and observe, poker-faced, then drift away. Or he'd come in, take a chair, and drum with us for a while. Then he and Etienne would go off on fantastic riffs together, and it was hard to concentrate on our simple patterns because theirs were so much more alluring.

I longed for the day when I would be promoted to the more complicated rhythms the advanced students played. Sometimes I even tried them, surreptitiously, I thought, though you cannot play an instrument surreptitiously; I'm sure my deviations didn't escape Etienne. I want to do what they're doing, I once said to him, and he nodded and smiled and said it would be very soon.

One day after class Etienne approached me and said that his regular students could pay him directly. I was surprised that he called me one of the regulars. I didn't feel like one of them yet. I could see that drumming and the drum school were part of the weave of their lives. They huddled together, talking about drumming sessions and performances, gossip and shop talk from a world remote from the one I knew. I came just once a week and still felt like an outsider as I stepped off the elevator; I felt the excitement and shyness of venturing into another country. Then I would retreat to my ordinary life that had nothing to do with drumming. Still, if Etienne considered me one of the regulars, I was pleased: the day couldn't be far off when I'd be playing the more complicated rhythms. Maybe I'd even start to come more often. Suddenly I was fantasizing, as I tend to do, about moving into an entirely new life: I could buy a drum, the other drummers would become my friends, I'd be part of their chatter, I'd go wherever they went after class and drum with them far into the night.

As I was taking up imaginary residence in the world of drumming, Etienne was explaining something about the class fees and seemed to be having trouble saying what he meant in English. I suggested that he speak French; this would be easier for him, but mostly I suggested it out of vanity. I wanted him to know I could understand and speak French, at least simple French if not the colloquial version the teachers spoke among themselves. In French, I gathered he was asking me to pay him for several classes in advance. An uneasy suspicion invaded my fantasies. His request was unusual, unbusinesslike. Then again, the school itself was not very businesslike. So unbusinesslike that I tended to forget it was a commercial enterprise, that Etienne was earning a living and I was purchasing his talent. If anything, I rather thought of myself as an initiate into an aesthetic discipline, at least for that weekly hour and a half—which might soon become more.

How come? I asked. Weren't we supposed to pay at the front desk? He mumbled that Christmas was coming and also he needed money to fix the cords on his drum. Those words struck my heart: his drum was a part of him, like a vital organ. They overrode my suspicion, made it seem stodgy and petty. If I truly was in another country, maybe things were done differently here. When in Rome... Besides, Etienne looked embarrassed to be telling me this, and I wanted to relieve him. He was the teacher, the gifted master; I didn't like seeing him humbled by need. It made him ordinary.

Yet even masters must have daily concerns, I thought. He was a young immigrant from Senegal making his way in a new country. He needed to fix the cords on his drum. My grandparents and my father had been immigrants and must have been in the same position, needing help. Of course I'd help him. But I had only about twenty-five dollars on me. I offered to give him a check. He said no, no check, but downstairs, in a convenience store a few doors away, was an ATM. We went together to find the ATM, I took out sixty dollars, enough for four classes, and Etienne thanked me. I asked whether I should still sign up at the desk next week and he said no, just come to class, everything would be fine.

The next week I realized that even though I'd paid for the class I still had to pay to rent the drum. When I explained this at the desk I was sharply rebuked; I shouldn't have paid Etienne directly, the woman said—that was not how things worked. Later, when she came around with her list, she had a nasty dispute with Etienne. We were drumming so I couldn't concentrate on all they said, but I knew I was the subject of this public dispute and I flushed, as if I'd been caught out in some shady dealing. Especially as I was still an outsider, not yet a true initiate, I felt ashamed. And then immediately irritated, both with the woman and with myself: I'd done nothing at all to be ashamed of. The woman's intrusion in our dim room was an affront, a harsh shaft of light from the practical world.

What was the problem? I asked Etienne after class. No problem, he said, everything would be fine. Next time I shouldn't sign in at the desk. I couldn't summon the French to explain about renting a drum, a banal technicality compared with the glories of drumming. Etienne played with such fierce integrity. The minor integrity of my paying three dollars to rent a drum shrank in comparison.

The next week I missed class. A compelling reason or just an excuse? I can't remember. I do remember that I anticipated—dreaded— another scene. Would I have to face disputes from now on? And why feel dread? Surely I was making too much of a trivial matter. Dread was, or should be, too strong a word for the situation. I thought of asking the regular students how they handled the fees, but I didn't know them well enough and didn't want to cause more trouble for Etienne. What was not trivial was that the spell of enchantment had been pierced.

The following week I didn't sign in at the front desk; I took a drum from the cabinet without paying. I didn't like doing that, but it seemed the simplest way. The class began and my hands quickly found the patterns. Etienne crooned. His hands flew. Another teacher ambled in with his drum and joined us. Amid the rapturous sounds of the drums, the world of commercial transactions shrank and fell away. I was a drummer, among other drummers.

But then the woman came around with her class list, tallying us up, and again there was a scene. This time I paid closer attention. Etienne was saying that these were *his* regular students, while the woman insisted that he must be paid through the school. I am so lacking in business sense that it hadn't occurred to me that the school, however informal it appeared, must have taken a sizable cut of the fifteen dollars. To Etienne this must have seemed unfair; it seemed unfair to me too, even if that was how things were done in my country.

Clearly I needed to straighten this out. I tried after class, but couldn't get my point across, in English or French. No, no, Etienne interrupted, there's no problem, you've already paid. He was packing up his drum for the day and seemed to be dismissing me. Other students were crowding around to speak to him. Daunted, I moved away.

I left, tangled in anger, guilt and impotence, a deadly brew. If only he had asked me for a loan to fix his drum—I would have given that willingly. But to avoid any such awkwardness, he had put me in the awkward position. I was angry too at the noisy woman with the list—the intruder—and at myself for failing to know how to settle the matter. Settling it should have been simple, and yet it was not. Worst of all, how banal the whole predicament was, compared with the drumming that filled the dark little room.

I tried to disentangle myself. Was this really worth fretting over? Why not pay at the desk as before, pretend I'd given him a gift to fix his drum? It wasn't the money, though; it was the injustice—and injustice is the same in any country. However helpless I felt, I wasn't willing to put up with it. Etienne had assured me there would be no problem, yet there was a problem. That was careless. And carelessness is vitiating in an artist—that was the same in any country too. It was unraveling the spell of the dim room.

Still, I thought, what I called careless was really a survival strategy: Etienne had done what immigrants have to do. I understood that. His life was no enchanted bubble. I might be the outsider in the drum class but I was at ease in my country. He was the outsider who had to make ends meet. Fix the cords on his drum. And to do so, on his territory he had made me the one called to account.

The next week, I didn't go to class, nor the weeks after that. It was winter now, cold and snowy; the subway trip was long. I couldn't muster the will. And for reasons I didn't fully understand, I didn't feel able to resolve this trivial issue, the kind of issue that outside the drum class, on my own territory, I could have handled easily. I felt excluded from the country that appeared when the elevator doors opened, as surely as if I'd been stopped at the border, my identity papers called into question.

Months later, one night on the subway, I found myself sitting next to a large, oval-shaped man in a dashiki and kofia. He was looking at me longer than one looks at strangers on the subway—the look of a man on the verge of striking up a conversation. I was amused: for a young African I'd be an unlikely choice for a subway pickup. Then I realized he was one of the teachers I'd seen so often in the lobby. I was the one who spoke first. Aren't you from the dance and drum school? I said. We greeted each other like old friends and he gave me news of the school. Why hadn't he seen me around lately? he wanted to know. So I'd been noticed. Maybe I might have become one of the regulars after all. I'd been very busy, I said. And how was Etienne? He was fine. Soon it was my stop. We shook hands warmly and I got off.

That made me think of returning to the class. By now the intensity had drained out of the incident. I'd forgotten about the money, never important anyway, and the injustice . . . well, it was too long ago to matter. I'd be glad to drum again in the dim little room and hear Etienne's fantastic riffs, watch his fingers fly till they blurred like the blades of a propeller. I could picture my return: the creaky elevator, the crowded lobby—a mini-Senegal—the sweating dancers through the wall of glass. The circle of chairs awaiting the drummers. Etienne would welcome me with a hug and exclamations and ask where I'd been for so long. I'd hug him back, but with a minuscule reservation— nothing he could detect, just a lingering grain of discomfort, like a stone in the shoe. A tiny, nagging pain, because I hadn't managed to set things right. Out of some diffidence I harbored, I had chosen to remain a tourist, an outsider. Or, more than diffidence, it was a stubborn knot in me—an exaggerated reverence for art tied up with guilt over race and privilege. So I had excluded myself from the other country. The other country, crowded, chaotic, relentlessly practical, couldn't afford such purity or soul-searching. It cut corners. Sometimes people got scraped in the process.

Of course you can walk even with a stone in your shoe, if you can't remove it and you really want or need to keep going. But I didn't keep going.

At least not then. A few years later—the whole incident nearly forgotten—I found another drum class, in a less exotic setting, where I don't feel like an outsider but like a student among other students. The teacher is quite as dazzling a performer as Etienne and, a native English speaker, explains the technique more clearly. From him I discovered how much more I still had to learn before I could become a true drummer: Etienne, I realized, had been too tolerant of my fumbling beginners' efforts. The new teacher is rigorous and demanding. But that is another story.

Maybe what I wanted back then was not so much the drumming, but an adventure, an adventure that, as it turned out, faltered at the first intrusion of troublesome reality, the first demand that I exert myself and claim my rights. Maybe I had gotten what I wanted, not a vocation but a vacation. A brief fantasy, a guided tour. Now I simply want to learn to play the drum.

Alone with the Cat

The cat was of no interest to me—I am not now and never was a cat lover. When cat lovers' cats made their advances, I sat in frozen courtesy. But for reasons also of no interest, I had to spend four months with the cat and I determined, on principle, to make something interesting out of our enforced sojourn. I studied the features of catness that cat lovers go on about with such ardor: the rippling undulations of flesh and fur, the ingenious forays into high and low places, the fabled inscrutabilities. I was impressed. The cat lovers were right about all that. On the other hand, the cat was not aloof, as cat lovers had led me to expect, but affectionate: like an infant, he craved attention.

I studied catness in stages, and soon I felt I had thoroughly witnessed its famous mysteries. Which is not to say that I plumbed those mysteries or that they were not worth plumbing, only that I had had enough: they were familiar now, and they were finite.

I might have passed the remaining time indifferent to the cat, but there came upon me an unfamiliar sense of freedom and power in his presence. Alone with the cat in this singular situation—not quite solitary, not quite social—I was free to do anything at all. He would never tell. The cat would not reveal any bursts of temper, peculiar lapses, eccentric habits or rituals, vexing flaws. If by any chance it judged, it would keep those judgments to itself and soon forget, or so I assumed; it would not bring old grudges to the next encounter as a person might.

Alone, we know who we are. In company our certainty is blurred. Other presences, like surgical lasers, penetrate and work subtle changes and adjustments on our innards. Also, in the company of others, we hide our faults as best we can or, failing that, tinge them with a whimsical, quasi-charming light, often deluding ourselves in the process. There is no need to hide our failings with a cat: the cat will never tell. With the cat I was not accountable, or not to anyone but myself. How I behaved with the cat would be a uniquely accurate reflection of character. Rather than penetrating and altering me, the cat would serve as my mirror.

Being with a baby comes to mind. Babies cannot tell, either. But with a baby we are constrained to behave decently since, after all, it is a baby and, more often than not, our own; moreover, if we behave badly with the baby, we may suffer the ill effects later on. We need not bear the ill effects of our behavior with a cat: if it becomes unmanageable or neurotic as a result of mistreatment, we can give it away, which is not ordinarily the case with a baby. So with a cat we see ourselves not through a gloss of social behavior but face to face, mirrored: who we really are in relation to the Other, who we might be in a situation of impossible freedom.

Under the unexpected aspect of mirror, the cat became infinitely fascinating, and my stay with him became an exercise in self-scrutiny—part of my routine in any event, and now accomplished while I cared for the cat. Killing two birds with one stone, as they say, only nothing like killing was involved. I was kind to the cat, for the most part; I had little urge to be cruel, even when he was intrusive or irritating. That was a happy discovery. I was willing to stroke and give the affection he craved, even willing to play a bit. But only when I was in the mood. I was utterly free, with the cat, to indulge my moods, which were many and various, a freedom I had not felt with babies. You cannot ignore babies when you are not in the mood, or rather, you can but you will suffer guilt or worse. You can ignore cats without suffering guilt, or at least I could. Did I hold myself to a higher standard of behavior with babies because babies are the same species and thus compel allegiance? Or was it simply greater love for the babies? I do not think greater love, though it surely existed, is the answer. Great love has never held anyone to a high standard of behavior; quite the contrary. At any rate, I was kind to the cat when I felt like it and ignored him when I felt no kindness, and these alternations were arbitrary.

Maybe not totally arbitrary. The moods of moody people do have causes, knotty but not beyond unraveling, should we care to unravel. Mine, at this stage, had nothing to do with the cat. They were strangely arbitrary. And when the cat seemed puzzled or dismayed at my arbitrariness I didn't care, as I would have with a baby; I would have cared what a baby thought of me, aside from caring for the baby itself. Faced with a baby's dismay I would have mustered a show of congeniality. With the cat I rarely made such efforts.

At first I was playful with the cat, and it loved to play. After a while I noticed that while I didn't mind having him curl up warm against my body, I no longer was inclined to play. I ought to play, I thought: the cat needed, or was entitled to, or at least would have enjoyed, play. But for various reasons, I no longer felt playful, and after some moral struggle, I decided I need not force myself to play with the cat as I surely would have done with a baby, who needs play for its civilized future.

So this cat would have to do without much play. He would be an infrequently played-with cat, and if his mood became somber in consequence, like mine, so be it. Failure to play was not mistreatment. Anyway, the cat would never tell.

If I was not obliged to play with him, I was even less obliged to sleep with him. Yet when he took to sleeping in my bed at night I liked feeling his ripply warmth nearby. I could even imagine myself a great-hearted cat lover, which I knew I was not. When he walked up my back and pawed at my face, though, I had no qualms about pushing him away. Qualms arose when he settled in the precise place at the end of the bed where I wanted to move my feet. The cat could not be faulted, yet my feet longed for that very spot. Why not just shove him over? The cat was sleeping. I have a keen reverence for sleepers; they seem so trusting and vulnerable, so touchingly benign in a near-sacred way, that I hate to disturb them. Still, it seemed overly scrupulous to sacrifice the comfort of my feet merely to avoid disturbing a cat, especially when in all likelihood he would promptly fall back asleep. On the other hand, who was I in the hierarchy of creatures, and of what importance were my feet, that this minuscule comfort should take precedence over the cat's sacred sleep? Wakeful and distracted, I pondered whether the need to move my feet might be born of a perverse, unconscious urge to cross the cat. No, I thought not. At last, overcome by the absurdity of self-denial, I would nudge him over. He looked innocently aggrieved and sometimes went away altogether. I wished I could explain and persuade him to return, only not to that precise spot. And his catty inability to grasp this explanation was frustrating and came between us.

Cat lovers say cats are a comfort, but I rarely found this to be so. Though his warmth at my side was pleasant, like a living pillow, the cat did not relieve loneliness or grief or frustration. Nor was he company; his cat silence, his very inability to tell, which conferred such freedom, was a drawback when it came to being company. The cat was more a burden than a comfort. As cat lovers are always saying, cats require little in the way of physical care, far less than infants. The burden was not physical care. The burden of the cat was its presence. It was there, inexorably, and as such demanded a response, whether attention or indifference. Even ignoring a fellow creature requires effort, and for the conscientious and scrupulous, possibly more effort than attention. But I made this effort. Now and then I regretted my inattentiveness and tried to make amends, treating the cat as I treat people, following the moral imperative that the needs of others have some claim on us, as we strive to believe. But only now and then, in an arbitrary way.

Physical care aside, the cat was a burden as infants are burdens and not company, except with infants we bear the burden as an investment in expectation of future returns: a baby will grow to be company, a comfort, while a cat, though it ages and endures, never outgrows catness. Besides, we are responsible for raising the babies, not only for their future good but for our own, since if we do not raise them properly, they will continue to be a burden. Also, people will readily see we have not raised our babies properly. Would people censure a cat's behavior and judge us to be poor cat raisers? I think not. The cat would be thought to have a bad nature. We would claim we had made every effort to raise it properly but its bad nature defeated our efforts. This excuse, rightly or wrongly, would not work with a child. The parents are held responsible. Nurture is more in vogue than nature.

Once, as I tried to nudge the cat off my desk—for he had the habit of leaping up to sit on my spread-out papers, a habit that was cute once or twice but soon palled—he slipped and landed not on his feet, as I had heard cats always do, but on his back. He looked stunned and distressed. I was distressed too, not only because I had had no intention of hurting him, but also because if he were maimed for life, I might be suspected of cruelty or violence. True, the cat could not tell—even if he could, my nudge had been gentle, not violent—but the vet might harbor suspicion. Mistakenly. Luckily, after a tense moment the cat rose and sauntered away.

On a few occasions I spoke harshly to the cat, but speaking harshly did not give the relief—often a false relief—that speaking harshly to a person might have given. In a moment of pique, I even smacked him lightly. And once, when the cat persisted in climbing on the kitchen counter, pawing and sniffing at food, knocking over containers, I screamed loudly, Get away. Get away! Twice, and louder than I had screamed at anyone or anything in years. My scream must have expressed a resentment stored up for some time, all the time I was learning the fabled mysteries of catness, a dormant resentment ready to spring awake and pounce. Maybe I had gained a measure of self-control since my screaming days, or maybe I grasped, even in my rage, that screaming would do no good: the cat could not understand a surge of bilious words as children would have done. Though now that I think of it, maybe they hadn't understood either, back then. Anyhow, no satisfaction could be gotten from scolding the cat, not that there is ever much satisfaction in scolding anyone, and somehow the opaque catness of the cat, the way it slunk away as if ashamed not of itself but of me, made that very clear.

I grasped that the presence of any living creature would be a burden to me, except maybe a plant. The least burdened state would be solitude, where I could indulge every arbitrary mood without the slightest thought for its effect on others. But solitude too has its burdens and demands. There is really no easy way to be conscious; that must be why I revere sleep.

I was cool toward the cat after the kitchen counter incident. Not cruel, only cool, again indulging my nature with all its moods. The cat would never tell. The cat might even be seen as practice for indulging my moods in society, for not straining to offer more in the way of kindness or encouragement than I am inclined to give. Cat therapy. I was almost afraid to envision how I might behave with people, were I to master too well the lessons of being with the cat. I would rarely consider how others felt or what they needed, until I was abandoned by everyone, left all alone to indulge my arbitrary moods.

After a day or so, I decided this coolness was unworthy of me. The cat was just a cat; it could not help climbing on the counter. (Or could it? Was it purposely provoking me? This is one of the unplumbed mysteries of catness.) It had no moral nature and apparently did not learn from experience; its feelings could be hurt, yes, but it was unwilling or unable to behave well in order to avoid having its feelings hurt. I had no illusion that cause and effect were operative, that shouting would deter him from pawing at food; I did not credit the cat with that much logic or self-control. Even babies do not have that much logic or self-control, though we tend to forget this when rearing them. Anyhow, the cat need not be prepared to get on in life. There were no crucial or obligatory lessons. Treating it well was in no way an investment in the future.

Treating the cat well was a gratuitous act. Living with the cat was living in an eternal present—no history, no patient shaping of connection through accommodation, nor any call for anger or forgiveness. The cat was a cat. I might as well end my coolness and give him the affection he craved. But I felt constrained giving affection I didn't feel, reasoned affection, so I waited a day or so until my annoyance dissipated and I could give affection in good faith, and we resumed our life in the eternal present.

In the end, I liked the cat best when he sat quietly on my lap and consented to being stroked. But while seemingly contented, he would abruptly leap up to pursue his mysterious business, as arbitrary in his way as I was in mine. Maybe he didn't like me at all, only used me as a provider of food and strokes. (Or as a mirror?) He must like me a bit, I thought. Probably he both liked me and used me, in very human fashion. We may love others, but they are useful all the same as providers, and it is wisest for both user and used not to measure comparative degrees of love and utility.

I remembered I loved my infants with most ease when they too lay docile on my lap, showing no will and making no abrupt movements. They were safe. Passive receptacles for my affection. I was safe. As soon as they stirred, perhaps to demand of me something unknown, I would feel a faint irritation that only years later I recognized as the mask of panic. As soon as a creature shows itself distinct and self-willed, it begins to determine and shape the nature of the love it seeks. And in turn, the love you give becomes something not entirely of your own shaping and thus dangerous. Was I unable, then, to love anything that had its own being; could I love only an utterly passive creature? If so, my love was arbitrary and self-serving, not so much love of something distinct from me as love of my own act of loving, which is easy, natural and demands nothing. Self-love.

The cat was becoming a fun-house mirror, alarming me with its unlovely distortions. I turned away. His usefulness was finished. Even so, when our sojourn was over, I missed the cat from the heart. I study photographs of him. In the photographs, there are no reflections of me. I see only the cat himself, large, orange and beautiful. At last, with him far away and requiring nothing, I can revel in his beauty.

ACKNOWLEDGMENTS

The essays listed below appeared in the following publications, sometimes in slightly different form: "This Is Where We Came In," "Wheelchair Yoga," "Absence Makes the Heart," "*Stone Reader*," and "Carlos Saura's *Cria!*" in *The Threepenny Review*; "'I Wish I Could Say the Same,'" "You Gotta Have Heart," and "The Piano" in *Agni*; "Meditations in Time of War" and "Reality Tour" in *Witness*; "Yes, New York, There Are Baby Pigeons" and "Street Food" in *The New York Times*; "Alone with the Cat" in *The American Scholar* and included in the collection *Face to Face*; "Listening to Anthony Powell" in *Salmagundi* and included in *Face to Face*; "Intimacy. Anger" in *Narrative*. "Ultimate Peek-a-boo" was included in the anthology *Eye of My Heart*, and "Heinrich Mann's *Man of Straw*" in the anthology *Rediscoveries*.